D0492831

THE ART
OF
EMBROIDERY

THE ART OF OF EMBROIDERY

JULIA BARTON

MEREHURST
LONDON

To my parents

Published 1989 by Merehurst Limited
Ferry House
51–57 Lacy Road
Putney
London SW15 1PR

Reprinted 1990 (twice)

Edited by Eleanor Van Zandt
Designed by Bill Mason
Photography by Stewart Grant and those listed on page 142
Artworks by Lindsay Blow
Drawings by Marie Linklater
Typesetting by Rowland Phototypesetting Limited, Bury St Edmunds, Suffolk
Colour separation by Fotographics Limited, London–Hong Kong
Printed in Belgium by Proost International Book Production, Turnhout

CONTENTS

INTRODUCTION   7

HISTORICAL DEVELOPMENT   8

MATERIALS *and* EQUIPMENT   14

DESIGN: Sources *and* Approaches   26

COLOUR   36

DRAWING *and* PAINTING   44

From DESIGN *to* EMBROIDERY   50

STITCHERY   58

FLAT PATTERN DESIGNS   78

QUILTING   80

APPLIQUÉ   88

MACHINE EMBROIDERY   94

JEWELLERY *and* ORNAMENTS   116

PRACTICAL INFORMATION   133

SUPPLIERS   140

For FURTHER READING   141

ACKNOWLEDGMENTS   142

INDEX   143

INTRODUCTION

This is a book for every aspiring embroiderer. Whether or not you have any experience in needlework, if you are fascinated by the colours and textures of fabrics and threads, you can learn to do creative, exciting work in this medium.

You may already enjoy doing the type of embroidery in which the design comes printed on the fabric and you are supplied with the threads to work it. However, the time will come when you wish to break away from this rather safe method of working and try choosing your own fabrics, threads and design sources. Throughout this book you will find various methods of developing your choice of design, from the first snapshot or drawing right through to the finished piece of embroidery.

Designing is an aspect of embroidery that most people find extremely daunting. I hope to show you that it need not be so. Inspiration for embroidery lies all around you, and with the help of a camera you can find patterns of line, shape and texture that can be successfully interpreted in embroidery. An understanding of colour and how colours interact will help you to plan your design; and so I have included a section on this fascinating yet — for many people — problematical subject, including a few simple exercises that will encourage you to enjoy using colour for its own sake.

Getting from the design source to the design itself can seem a formidable challenge. However, there are many ways of approaching design. Simple cut-paper shapes can be developed into flat patterns suitable for quilting and appliqué; and tracings from photographs can be enlarged and used as the basis for pictorial or abstract work. Many embroiderers are frightened by drawing, but I hope to demonstrate that you can learn to handle drawing media well enough to put your design ideas onto paper in usable form. I also show you some different ways to get the design onto the fabric, by using one of the traditional methods or by using fabric paints. These new products have created many possibilities for embroiderers and are especially useful in providing a structure on which to build the finished design.

The art of embroidery embraces many different techniques, each with its own distinctive character. For this book I have chosen some of the most enduringly popular, as well as some new ones. Stitchery, of course, lies at the heart of embroidery; but today stitches are not used merely to fill in patterns but to create a wealth of exciting textures. Hand stitchery is often combined with machine embroidery, whose wonderfully spontaneous quality is being exploited so imaginatively these days. Traditional favourites such as quilting and appliqué are also appearing in new guises.

One of the newest developments in embroidery is textile jewellery. I have included a section on this subject which I hope will encourage you to be adventurous and create your own original jewellery in fabric and thread.

Historical Development

TRADITIONS OF EMBROIDERY

The art of decorating textiles is almost as old as the human race; and the study of its history affords a fascinating insight into the social, economic and religious aspects of art and design throughout the centuries. Embroidery has been used in countless ways and for many different purposes: to embellish elaborate trousseaux and funerary wrappings, to proclaim the glory of God and the majesty of kings, to add a little colour to the simple homes of peasants and to display great wealth.

In Europe, the Middle Ages saw a great flowering of ecclesiastical embroidery – none more beautiful than *opus anglicanum*, or 'English work'. Created by professional designers and embroiderers in London workshops, *opus anglicanum* was worked in silk and gold threads and is char-

acterized by exceptionally fine detail and complex pictorial designs. The finest of this work was produced between 1250 and 1350. The work was so highly prized that it was given as gifts by visiting kings and emperors.

During the Renaissance, embroidery was increasingly used for secular purposes. Royalty and nobility wore elaborate clothing, richly encrusted with silk embroidery, jewels and spangles. In sixteenth-century Spain and England, a fashionable type of embroidery was blackwork, a counted-thread technique using a variety of complex patterns. Chair coverings, table carpets and wall hangings were often embroidered in canvas work (now also called needlepoint), using silk thread on fine linen canvas.

The custom of embroidering home furnishings became even more widespread in the seventeenth century. The work was often done by amateurs,

Left: This portrait of an English lady, Mary Cornwallis, painted by George Gower (1540–96), shows the Elizabethans' love of richly embroidered clothing. The splendid sleeves are embroidered in blackwork, a fashion believed to have originated in Spain, and veiled with fine lawn.

Opposite: The Syon Cope is one of the most beautiful surviving examples of opus anglicanum. *Its intricately detailed images of Christ, saints and angels are worked in silk and gold threads.*

Below: This detail from a sixteenth-century Swiss wall hanging shows an amateur embroiderer (Luigia Morell) working on a frame. Wool, silk, linen and metal threads are included in the work.

using designs taken from pattern books. There was a strong Oriental influence, due to trade with the Far East, and motifs such as exotic birds and flowers figured prominently in the newly popular technique of crewel work, which consisted of swirling designs executed in worsted woollen threads on a linen or cotton background fabric.

The techniques of crewel work and canvas work travelled from Britain to North America with the early settlers. There, the techniques were sometimes adapted slightly, mainly to save the expensive imported materials; for example, a one-sided version of satin stitch was often used instead of the traditional two-sided version.

Very little of the embroidery produced in the Colonies was worked in silk, which was extremely scarce and costly. In Europe, however, silk embroidery continued to flourish throughout the eighteenth century. Worked by professionals, in

Left: This detail from a set of bed hangings embroidered in silk and gold threads, shows eighteenth-century Chinese embroidery at its most spectacular. The hangings, along with the state bed for which they were made, were discovered in 1984 at Calke Abbey, Derbyshire, packed away in a trunk. Believed to have been a present from the British Royal Family, received in the 1730s, they had, incredibly, never been used — which accounts for their astonishing state of preservation.

designs of great intricacy, it featured subtle, realistic shading effects, achieved with long-and-short stitch, and was used extensively to decorate the formal dress of ladies and gentlemen.

One of the main factors affecting the type of embroidery native to a particular country has been the kinds of materials available locally. This is the reason why China, where silkworms were first cultivated, developed a tradition of exquisite silk embroidery long before this valuable thread reached Europe, via the 'silk route', during the Middle Ages. The climate of northern Europe encouraged the growing of flax, a strong fibre

which lends itself well to drawn- and pulled-thread work — types of embroidery in which this region has excelled. Similarly, crewel work was stimulated partly by the thriving British wool trade. Cotton is grown in warmer climates and is thus found in areas such as Egypt, the American South and India. The fine muslin produced in India inspired the technique of tambour work, in which chain stitch is worked with a crochet hook.

As trade has expanded, making an ever-wider range of materials available throughout the world, embroiderers in different countries have expanded their variety of techniques and styles.

TWENTIETH-CENTURY EMBROIDERY

During the past 20 years, there has been a great upsurge of interest and innovation in the art of embroidery. This is especially true in Britain, where the subject is now widely taught in art colleges and, increasingly, in secondary schools. Many of today's well-known embroiderers and teachers have had an art training, which helps to maintain a high standard of design teaching and is gradually raising embroidery from its previous status as a craft to that of an art form. Adult education classes on embroidery have proved ex-

tremely popular; and the growing interest in the subject has also been stimulated by the showing of embroidery on television, an increase in the number of books on embroidery and, in Britain, by the activities of the Embroiderers' Guild, which organizes frequent exhibitions and promotes embroidery on a national and an international level.

Embroidery today is extremely versatile and inventive. Modern embroiderers use a wide variety of fabrics and threads, some of them far from conventional. Many different media are employed, including hand-made papers, fabrics stif-

Right: This panel by Richard Box, one of Britain's foremost embroiderers, is based on a painting of wisteria and incorporates fabric collage and machine and hand embroidery.

Below: a panel, 'Tuscan Study I', by Jenni Last. This embroidery was inspired by a stone wall in Florence. Fragments of silk fabric, some painted, and knitting have been applied to gauze (partially cut away) to create subtle harmonies of colour and texture.

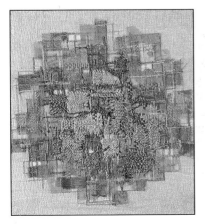

fened with plaster, wire and other found objects. At times, this has deteriorated to produce a gimmicky effect; but the sensitive use of such materials gives some modern embroidery great originality and impact.

One of the main developments in contemporary embroidery is the extensive use of fabric paints to colour both fabrics and threads. These paints are very popular in Britain, where they are used in conjunction with many different embroidery techniques, and in the United States, where they have proved ideal for creating interesting fabrics for quilt-making. Another important development is the increasing popularity of machine embroidery. Both of these techniques have a spontaneous quality which — along with their relative speed — makes them well-suited to modern tastes and lifestyles. They also combine happily with hand stitchery. The hand stitches worked by modern embroiderers have a free, adventurous character totally unlike traditional work; but even today they remain the essence of the art.

Left: This panel by Verina Warren, entitled 'The Silver Depths of Stillness Lie', incorporates machine embroidery and fabric paints, some applied with an airbrush. The larger scale of the stitching on the mount enhances the three-dimensional quality of the work.

Left: Varied materials, including silk organza, paper, plaster and dyes, were used by Stephanie Tuckwell for this abstract piece of embroidery.

Opposite: 'Colour Sound — Garden Light — September', by Julia Caprara, exemplifies this embroiderer's love of intense colour. Sheer fabrics and a variety of hand stitches, including buttonhole and free-standing loops (deliberately mis-formed French knots) appear to grow out of the painted wooden board.

Right: a detail from a panel, 'In My Craft or Sullen Art', by Eleri Mills, which was inspired partly by the poem of that name by Dylan Thomas.

MATERIALS *and* EQUIPMENT

There is such a wealth of materials and equipment available to today's embroiderer that it is easy to get carried away completely and buy anything and everything that appeals. Fortunately, though, embroidery is a relatively inexpensive pursuit; and it is possible to achieve satisfactory results with quite basic equipment.

I have divided the materials you will need into the following categories:

- Materials for design
- Fabric paints and dyes
- Fabrics
- Threads
- Sewing equipment.

You will not need to buy all the items listed immediately (in fact, you will build up your supply of fabrics and threads gradually), but most of them will be useful at one time or another.

MATERIALS FOR DESIGN

PAPER You will need a selection of different papers for different purposes.

A sketchbook of good cartridge (drawing) paper is extremely useful for practising drawing and making notes; you can also insert in its pages samples of fabrics and threads that might be used for future projects. Ideas are easily forgotten if you do not keep a record of them.

Watercolour paper is useful for exercises using paints and inks. However, it is not essential, as good-quality cartridge (drawing) paper makes an adequate substitute.

Coloured papers   Children's coloured 'play paper' (construction paper) is usually available from toy shops and is very useful for making cut-paper designs.

Opposite: a sketchbook and assorted coloured papers.
Above: a variety of drawing media.

Coloured tissue can be used for designing; several shapes can be cut out at once and arranged in a repeating pattern or overlapped for a subtle effect.

Magazine papers   Coloured pages from magazines, such as the backgrounds to advertisements, provide many subtle variations of colour. They can be used to construct colour schemes, and also for cut-paper shapes when designing for quilting or appliqué.

Tracing paper   This is useful for tracing interesting details from photographs or books. Good tracing paper can be bought from art shops; cheaper quality, in stationery departments (in Britain, greaseproof paper is a good alternative).

DRAWING MATERIALS

Pencils are available in many different grades, according to the softness of the lead. H grades are harder than B grades; the higher the number, the greater the degree of hardness or softness. For most purposes a B and a 2B will be adequate.

Charcoal and *Conté crayons* are softer drawing media and are very useful for bold work. They are excellent for the beginner to try, but will need fixing with an aerosol fixative to prevent them from smudging.

Charcoal pencils are less messy to use than charcoal and are available in a wide range of colours. Because they are in pencil form, they are less suitable for the beginner than the freer medium of soft pastels.

Coloured pencils are available from art shops. The most useful type are those which are used dry and then wetted with a brush dipped in water to give a watercolour effect. The extra-thick coloured pencils, over which one has less fine control, are especially recommended. Some lovely effects can be achieved with a damp brush or sponge after the colours have been applied to the paper.

Pastels consist of colour pigments, chalk and pipe clay. They are available in a large selection of colours because they are not usually mixed on the paper. However, it is possible to blend them quite easily by overlaying the colours and then rubbing the powder with a cotton bud (Q-tip) or your finger.

Oil pastels appear to be more like wax crayons, but they are just pastel powder mixed with oil. They give a bold effect, and colours can be blended by overlaying them on the paper. For a softer effect, white (mineral) spirit can be added with a cotton bud (Q-tip) or a small piece of cotton wool (absorbent cotton).

Right: drawing ink, watercolour and gouache paint and brushes, sizes 2 and 8.

Opposite: an assortment of design materials.

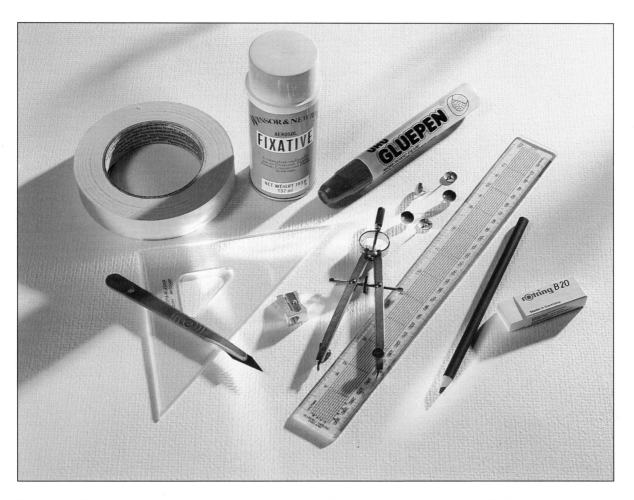

PAINTS These are usually divided broadly into watercolours, oils and acrylics. The latter two media are rather beyond the scope of designing for embroidery. Oils, in particular, are very slow to dry, and they have a built-in disadvantage for embroidery in that their 'painterly' quality tends to give finished pictures rather than material for a design. However, both oils and acrylics have a textured quality, analogous to that of a decorated textile surface, and thus might suggest effects that could be interpreted in stitchery.

Artists' watercolour paints contain no chalk or opaque material, which makes them completely translucent when used.

Gouache paint, which comes in tubes, is an opaque watercolour paint and is a medium often chosen by designers. Only a few basic colours are needed, as they will intermix and can be watered down to any shade and density required.

Coloured inks, which are available from art shops, are clear and liquid and come in bright colours. For deeper colour, several layers of ink can be applied.

BRUSHES Good brushes can be very expensive, but a well-stocked art shop should have a cheaper range, which will be perfectly adequate. A reasonable range of sizes would be: 2 (small), 4 (medium) and 6–8 (large). A small real sponge and a car-washing sponge to cut up will also be very useful for applying paints.

There are several other useful items of design equipment, some of which you may already have. These include a ruler, a set square (right-angled triangle), drawing pins (thumbtacks), glue, masking tape, a compass, a rubber (eraser), a pencil sharpener, a craft knife and a can of aerosol fixative for pastels.

Right: fabric paints and markers, applied to wet and dry fabric. 'Permanent' paints are shown at far right; liquid paints, centre; markers, right.

Opposite: transfer paints printed onto natural fabric (top) and synthetic fabric (centre right), showing how the colour differs from the original (centre left). The transfer crayon marks (bottom left) are fainter on the fabric.

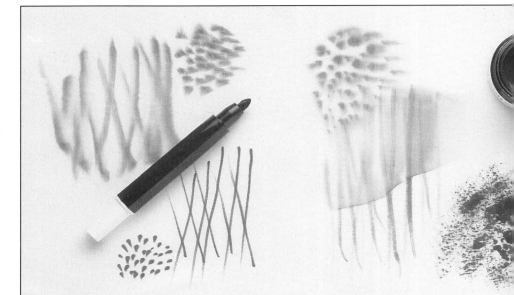

FABRIC PAINTS AND DYES

There are so many new products on the market that are designed to colour fabrics that it is almost impossible to know what to choose. The following descriptions of the different types should give you some idea of which will be most useful for the kind of work you are doing at a particular time.

FABRIC PAINTS   Sometimes called 'permanent fabric paints', these products are the most widely available and the easiest to use. They are painted or printed directly onto the fabric with a brush or sponge. Some, such as Color-Fun, have a liquid consistency; others, such as those manufactured by Pelikan, are paste-like in texture. They can all be thinned down and sprayed onto the fabric with a diffuser or an airbrush. Once fixed, they are permanent.

LIQUID FABRIC PAINTS   Also called 'silk paints', because they were developed for use on silk, these can, in fact, be used on almost any fabric. They are much more free-flowing than ordinary fabric paints, and tend to spread on the fabric. If you wish to prevent this, you can first outline the shape with a resist; the colour will then spread only as far as the outline. The resist is available in a clear form, which washes out, and in some colours, including metallic shades, with which some lovely results can be achieved.

FABRIC MARKERS   These look like felt-tip pens but are designed to be used on fabrics. They tend to make rather linear marks, but will give a softer effect if the fabric is wet.

The paints and markers described above are all set by ironing on the reverse of the fabric. After ironing, the design is completely washable and colourfast.

TRANSFER PAINTS   These paints are first painted onto a piece of paper; then the design is ironed off onto the fabric. Transfer paints are most effective on synthetic fabrics, such as nylon or polyester, and on natural synthetic mixtures. They do not give such a vibrant effect on fabrics made of natural fibres, such as cotton, linen and silk.

TRANSFER CRAYONS   These crayons are used in basically the same way as transfer paints, and, like them, work best on synthetics. The colours tend to be rather bright, but can be mixed on the paper to give a more subtle effect. Transfer crayons are particularly effective when used for rubbings. When ironed onto fabric, the resulting designs are especially suitable for English quilting, shadow quilting and machine embroidery.

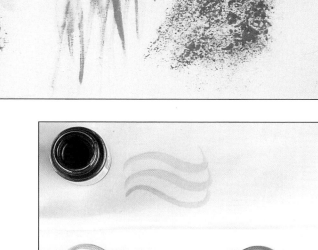

FABRICS

Almost any fabric is potentially useful for embroidery. In fact, one of the most exciting aspects of embroidery today is the enormous range of fabrics available and the ingenious uses modern embroiderers find for them. Once you begin designing your own embroidery you will find yourself collecting and hoarding all sorts of materials, from old nylon stockings to upholstery fabric.

Broadly speaking, fabrics for embroidery can be divided into the following categories, depending upon their uses:

- background fabrics
- fabrics for appliqué
- evenweave fabrics.

BACKGROUND FABRICS   The most important consideration in choosing a background fabric is that it must be suitable for the type of embroidery that you are going to do.

For large panels and hangings, hessian (burlap) and heavy-duty furnishing fabrics are suitable. They will take the weight of whatever is applied to them; and some are sufficiently loosely woven to allow thick threads to be used.

For small panels, in which finer threads might be used, a lighter, more closely woven furnishing fabric or a plain-weave embroidery linen would be suitable.

Backgrounds for machine embroidery are typically closely woven fabrics, such as cotton poplin or calico (unbleached muslin).

Another fabric well suited to stitchery is felt. This is usually available from craft shops in a selection of colours, but it can also be obtained in white, specially prepared for dyeing, from some mail order firms (see Suppliers, page 140). It has a soft quality which is suitable for both hand and machine stitching.

DYES   There are also a number of different kinds of dye on the market. These are generally intended for dyeing garments but can equally well be used for dyeing fabrics and threads for embroidery. Make sure to buy the appropriate product for the fibre content of the material you are dyeing.

FABRICS FOR APPLIQUÉ   This category includes any fabric that can be applied to the background, either to add a different texture or, in the case of transparent fabrics, to create veiled or subtle relief effects. Almost any fabric can be used for appliqué, the only limitation being the weight

BACKGROUND FABRICS

APPLIQUÉ FABRICS

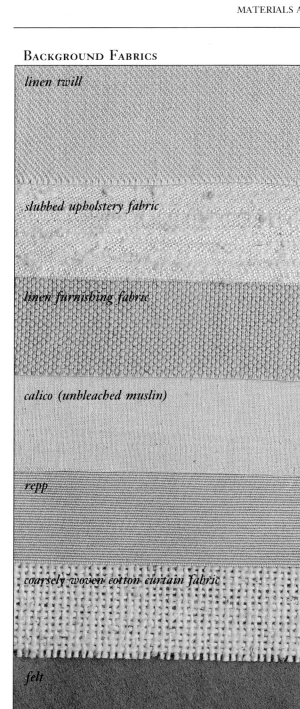

linen twill

slubbed upholstery fabric

linen furnishing fabric

calico (unbleached muslin)

repp

coarsely woven cotton curtain fabric

felt

hessian (burlap)

gauze

gold lamé

ribbed silk

net

cotton velvet

wool voile

synthetic scrim

silk organza

rayon satin

acrylic curtain fabric

raw silk

of the background fabric, which must be firm enough to support the fabric applied to it.

Transparent fabrics, such as chiffon, net, voile and organza, can all be used to provide sheer layers in a design. They can be ruched and gathered before being sewn to the background, or they can be applied in flat layers to give shadowy effects. Slightly thicker fabrics, such as fine linen scrim, cotton scrim and medical gauze, can be pulled into holes before being applied over other layers of fabric.

Opaque fabrics are also very useful for appliqué, especially where specific textures are required. For instance, a piece of green satin or velvet might be chosen because it suggests the texture of a particular leaf; or a piece of thin, worn-looking leather might be suitable for interpreting part of a stone wall. The choice of fabric will depend on the texture required and on the use of the finished embroidery. Consideration must be given to the washability and general care of the fabric, particularly in the case of household objects such as cushions and bed-covers.

EVENWEAVE FABRICS This kind of fabric has the same number of threads per centimetre (or inch) in both directions — that is, in both warp and weft. It comes in various weights, from 14 to 36 threads per 2.5 cm (1 inch) and is usually of cotton or linen. Evenweave fabrics are used mainly for counted-thread techniques, in which it is important not only that the threads can be easily counted but also that they form a square grid, so that the patterns created by the stitches will not be distorted.

Single thread evenweave can be used for any counted-thread embroidery, and is especially suitable for drawn-thread work, pulled work and pattern darning. Double thread evenweave, such as the relatively coarse Aida cloth, is often used for cross-stitch and blackwork embroidery. A finer double evenweave fabric, called Hardanger fabric, is designed especially for the traditional Norwegian embroidery of that name.

This technique and the other counted-thread styles of embroidery lie outside the scope of this book; however you may sometimes find evenweave fabrics useful as backgrounds for free stitchery or as materials for appliqué.

EVENWEAVE FABRICS

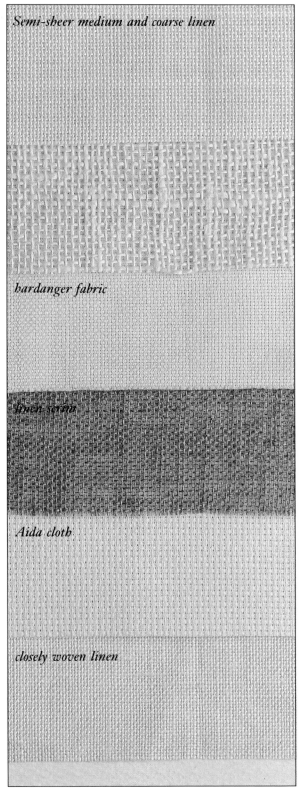

Semi-sheer medium and coarse linen

hardanger fabric

linen scrim

Aida cloth

closely woven linen

THREADS

Almost any kind of thread can be used for embroidery today. The only restriction in choosing threads for working is that they should be suitable for the fabric and for the type of embroidery. It is worthwhile collecting together as many different threads as possible. Knitting yarn shops often have a basket containing ends of lines, which are usually a fraction of the original price. A friend who knits may also have some leftover yarn to spare. Some of the metallic yarns used in crochet and knitwear, depending on the fashion, can enliven the surface of your embroidery — as can the fine metallic threads intended for machine work.

Aim for the greatest possible variety: thick and thin, matt and shiny. If you store them according to colour, you will find them much more convenient to use than if stored according to type. Clear containers will make it easier to see what you've got. The big plastic jars used in sweet shops in Britain are ideal; see if the shopkeeper will let you have his empty ones.

You may not be fortunate enough to have a good specialist embroidery shop near you, but there are many mail order companies, whose addresses are to be found in embroidery and craft magazines (as well as on page 140 of this book).

WOOL THREADS

Tapestry wool   This is a thick, matt thread traditionally used for canvas work (needlepoint).
Crewel wool   This strong, fine wool thread was traditionally used for crewel work. It can be used in several strands for canvas work (needlepoint), but when used for surface stitchery, it gives a better effect when used singly.
Persian wool   This consists of three easily separated strands of yarn, somewhat thicker than crewel and thinner than tapestry. It is used for both canvas work and surface embroidery.

COTTON THREADS

Perlé cotton   Also called *coton perlé* or pearl cotton, this thick, twisted, lustrous thread is lovely to use. It is available in three thicknesses, numbers 3, 5 and 8 (the finest). No. 5 is the most popular and comes in the greatest variety of colours.
Coton à broder   This is a single thickness, smooth, lustrous thread which is particularly suitable for counted-thread work.
Stranded cotton (embroidery floss)   This consists of six strands, which can be used singly or combined as required.
Soft (matte) embroidery cotton   This is almost the only matt thread in the cotton range. It is very thick and most effective for large-scale work.
Machine embroidery threads   These come in two thicknesses, sizes 30 and 50. No. 30 is the thicker of the two and easier to use.

LINEN THREADS   These are usually available from lacemakers' suppliers. They are the threads traditionally used on evenweave linen for counted-thread work. Although available only in a limited colour range, they are easy to dye.

SILK THREADS

Silk buttonhole twist   Unfortunately, this is almost impossible to find anymore, but if you have some left over from dressmaking, you might consider using it to add a bit of lustre to an embroidery.
Silk sewing thread   This can be found in haberdashery (notions) departments. It is often used in machine embroidery. A much larger range of silk threads in wonderful colours can be obtained from some mail-order suppliers.

RAYON THREADS

Hand embroidery threads   These highly lustrous threads, some stranded and lightly spun and some single-filament, are available from some embroidery shops and mail-order companies.
Machine embroidery threads are also very shiny. These come in a large colour range, usually from a mail-order supplier.

Some of the many threads that can be used for embroidery. From upper left downwards: extra-fine ribbon, two reels of machine embroidery thread and one of silk thread, two skeins of perlé cotton, two skeins each of soft embroidery cotton and French crewel wool. From upper right downwards: two skeins of stranded cotton floss and one of stranded rayon thread, a skein of linen thread, two skeins of coton à broder, metallic embroidery thread, and one skein each of crewel wool, soft embroidery cotton, silk knitting yarn, Persian wool and tapestry wool.

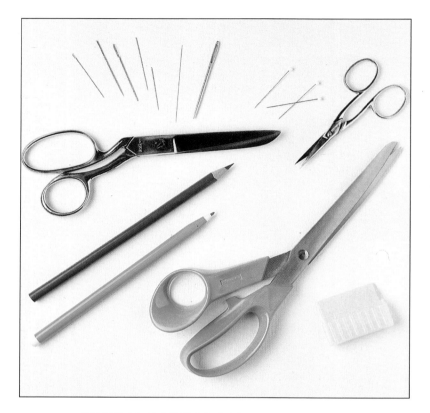

A selection of sewing equipment including needles (from left, crewel, chenille, tapestry, sharp, between, beading and rug), an embroidery transfer pencil, a water-erasable marker and tailor's chalk.

SEWING EQUIPMENT

SCISSORS Three pairs of scissors are essential: one large pair for cutting fabrics, one small, fine-pointed pair for cutting threads, and an old pair for cutting paper.

NEEDLES
Crewel A sharp needle with a long eye, available in many sizes, suitable for a variety of threads.
Chenille A needle with a relatively large eye which (in the larger sizes) will take very thick threads. Also called a heavy embroidery needle.
Tapestry A needle with a blunt point, available in different thicknesses; used mainly in counted-thread work and canvas work (needlepoint), but also for some free embroidery stitches.
Sharp A fine needle for use with sewing threads.
Between Similar to sharp, but comparatively short; often used for hand quilting.
Beading A very fine, long needle, used mainly for stitching on beads.
Rug A very large needle with a blunt point, for use on rug canvas.

PINS Steel dressmakers' pins are the best to use. Glass-headed pins are longer and are very useful for thick fabrics and for quilting.

FABRIC MARKERS
Water-erasable marker Often called a 'quilters' pen', this can be used to mark the design directly onto the fabric. After the embroidery is worked, the marks are removed by sponging with water. Another type of pen, whose mark fades in the air, is better for delicate fabrics. In any case, these pens should be tested on the fabric before use.
Embroidery transfer pencil This is used for drawing the design onto paper; the design is then ironed off onto the fabric. Some of these pencils tend to smudge, and the mark is not always easy to remove afterwards; so this method needs to be used with caution.
Tailor's chalk This is an old-fashioned method of marking fabric, but it is still very useful today, since the mark is easy to remove. It is normally used only for temporary marking before a more permanent mark, such as tacking (basting) is made.

FRAMES   For most types of embroidery, you will need to use a frame, in order to hold the fabric taut. Frames vary considerably in size, type and price; the choice of frame in a particular case will depend on the type of embroidery being worked. It is advisable, in hand embroidery, to choose a frame that will accommodate the whole area to be embroidered. This enables work to progress on the whole piece at once and prevents the work from becoming marked or creased by the frame. Instructions for using embroidery frames are given on page 133.

Round or tambour frames are particularly useful for machine embroidery and small pieces of hand stitching. The traditional tambour frame consists of two wooden rings, the outer ring having a tightening screw to enable the fabric to be gripped tightly. Some tambour frames are equipped with a clamp which is attached to a table, leaving both hands free for working. Another type has a flat base on which the embroiderer sits. Standing tambour frames are also available. A special type of tambour frame, used for machine embroidery, is described on page 95.

Rectangular frames   These consist of four strips of wood joined to form a rectangle. The simplest type can be made from four strips of fairly soft wood, such as pine, measuring about 2.5 by 1.5 cm (1 by ½ inch) in section. These are joined with wood glue and held rigid by four flat right-angle brackets. A slightly more sophisticated version has mitred corners, which are glued and nailed together like a picture frame. In art supply shops you can buy canvas stretchers with mitred corners, which are slotted together. Alternatively, an old picture frame can be used.

Slate frames, also called *scroll frames*, are adjustable wooden frames. They vary slightly in their construction, but a common type consists of two rollers with webbing attached and two strips or laths which hold the rollers at the chosen distance. Although the work cannot be wider than the length of the webbing strips, it can be longer than the side strips; the excess is rolled over the rollers and then unrolled as required. Some slate frames can be attached to a table or floor stand. The method of mounting the fabric (see page 133) allows it to be re-tautened if necessary.

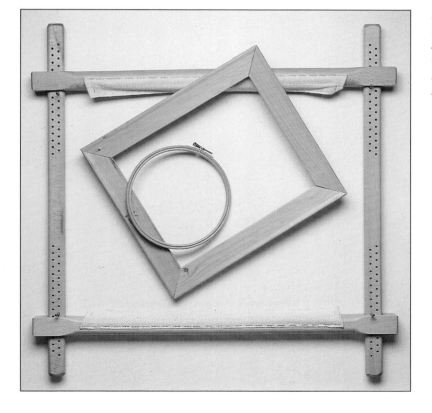

Left: the three basic types of embroidery frame: an adjustable slate frame, a rectanglar frame made from canvas stretchers, and a ring frame with an adjustable screw.

DESIGN: SOURCES *and* APPROACHES

There are many ways of designing for embroidery. The method chosen in a given case may depend on the function of the finished item (whether, for example, the design must fit into a certain shape); on the technique or materials to be used; and on the original source of inspiration for the design. Some people find it possible to stitch directly from observation, and this approach can lead to a spontaneous and lively piece of work. It is also possible to work directly from a photograph or drawing, provided that there is enough visual information in the source to serve as a basis for the stitchery.

More often, the source is first adapted in some way — for example, by means of making a sketch or cutting and arranging paper shapes. These design techniques are discussed on pages 48 and 78 respectively. Here, I shall concentrate on the source material itself and also show you two simple methods of deriving designs from it.

SOURCES OF INSPIRATION   The first thing to do is to become keenly aware of your surroundings. It does not matter whether you are indoors, in the garden or in the middle of a field. You will need to look, touch, smell, and even listen, in order to take in as much information as possible about your subject. Sometimes we take our senses for granted and see only what we think we see. By contrast, a small child will poke his finger into a hole to find out what is inside, or will run his fingers over a rough surface to confirm what his eyes tell him. We should train ourselves to be equally inquisitive about our surroundings, in order to find subjects suitable for embroidery designs.

To help you to 'see' these subjects, I have chosen three sources of visual material: landscape, texture and museum exhibits. As you develop your powers of observation you will find others.

LANDSCAPE

The general category of landscape includes many different kinds of subject, such as mountains, gardens, forests and open countryside with farmhouses and other buildings. Books, magazines, calendars and postcards can provide innumerable photographs of landscapes and gardens that could serve as source material. Another possibility is to take your own pictures. By using your own camera you can choose your own subjects.

An endless variety of subject matter can be found in landscapes. The horizontal and diagonal lines in this Tuscan landscape (right); the subtly coloured, interlocking shapes — natural and man-made — on a Greek island (Santorini, below); and the contrasting shapes and variety of scale in a Norwegian mountain scene (left) show the range of possibilities. Seascapes, too, offer fascinating patterns and textures, as this view (lower right) illustrates.

Your first look through the viewfinder will probably be a general one with more of the middle and far distance in view than details of the foreground. Take several shots of this view, moving the camera between each shot so that you include different groupings of trees, for example, or change the position of the horizon line.

Now look more closely at the foreground; this may involve sitting or even lying on the ground, so that whatever is in the foreground takes up the whole picture. In some cases this will produce an image in which the stems or foliage in the foreground form a natural frame for the distant landscape, so that the view has depth. You might want to show both foreground and background in some detail; or you might prefer to show only one plane clearly. If it is possible to alter the settings on the camera, it is quite an easy matter to choose which part of your photograph is to be in focus and to blur out the remainder. Focus on your chosen

area, then select a large aperture such as F4 or F5.6, and, if necessary, a short time setting to compensate. This will have the effect of reducing the depth of field, allowing only your chosen area to be in focus.

SELECTING AN AREA When your photograph is printed, you may still need to select a particular area to work from, so that you avoid including too much complicated detail. Take a piece of fairly stiff paper, and from it cut two L-shaped strips. (If you make them reasonably large — say, to fit within this page — you will be able to use them with a

Left: Paper L-strips are shown on a photograph of a poppy field enclosing the area chosen as the basis for an embroidery design. Notice how the photographer has shot the scene from a low angle, so as to get as much detail as possible.

variety of different sources.) Move the strips over the photograph until they enclose an area that forms an attractive subject for the embroidery. Mark the edges of the chosen area, and then trace the image.

ENLARGING THE DESIGN   Your traced image will probably be quite small, and will need to be enlarged to the desired size. It may be possible to have this done photographically; simply tape the tracing to a piece of opaque paper, take it to a photocopying service and ask to have it enlarged to the required size. Alternatively, you can use the traditional method of proportional enlargement, sometimes called scaling up.

1. On top of the tracing, draw a grid of straight lines, with the help of a ruler. The easiest way to do this is to divide the area vertically and horizontally in half, then in quarters (if the design is complex, further divisions may be necessary).
2. Tape the tracing to the lower left-hand corner of a large sheet of paper. Decide on the desired vertical or horizontal measurement of the finished work (whichever is more

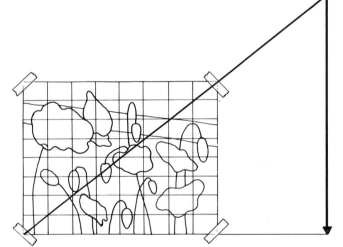

Left and below: stages in enlarging a design. When the height (or the width) of the enlarged design has been decided, a diagonal line is drawn up through the original to this level; then another line is drawn perpendicular to the base line (as shown by the arrow). Then the new rectangle is divided into the same number of sections as the original. Finally, the design is copied, square by square, onto the enlarged grid.

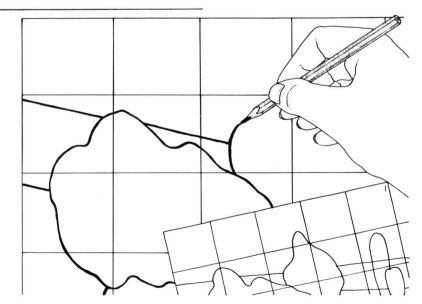

important), and draw a line along that side of the tracing, extending it to the desired measurement. Also extend the adjacent side by a generous amount.

3. Draw a diagonal straight line from the lower left to the upper right corner of the original, and extend this line to the new height (or width) measurement.

4. With the help of a set square (right-angled triangle), draw a line perpendicular to the measured line, crossing the diagonal. Draw another line from this crossing point down to the adjacent side. You now have a rectangle exactly proportional to the original tracing.

5. Divide the enlarged rectangle in the same way as you did the original, forming the same number of sections. For convenience, label the lines A, B, and 1, 2, etc. on both grids.

6. Now transfer the design onto the larger grid, section by section.
   This same method can also be used to reduce a design.

The full-size design can now be used as a basis for whatever type of embroidery you have in mind. For example, this poppy design was interpreted in free appliqué for the little panel shown below.

Below: This little panel, based on the enlarged tracing of the poppies, is worked in hand stitchery and appliqué, with red silk chiffon loosely gathered up to suggest the flowers.

TEXTURE

Having looked at landscape from a distance, you should now take a closer look at some of the details — in particular, at the wonderful range of textures it contains. You may need also to use your sense of touch to gain a full understanding of the rough, wrinkled texture of bark, for example, or the soft, velvety texture of moss growing on a dead tree stump.

You might like to try drawing or painting the textures that you can see, using some of the guidelines given on pages 45–48. A camera with a telephoto (close-up) lens is a useful piece of equipment when making these studies, but you can also find many marvellous photographs of textures, both coloured and black and white, in textbooks on the natural sciences and geology.

Select only the detailed areas of your subjects, so that you are conscious of the texture only and not of the whole object. Your detailed area should contain some contrasts, such as smooth and shiny contrasting with rough and bumpy. This will bring variety to your design and prevent it from having an overall sameness, which can be very dull.

Above and left: The contrasting textures to be found in the natural world are suggested by the smooth, undulating patterns on a rock face and some delicate, fuzzy wild flowers.

Ground-covering plants (right) and old stone walls (below) offer other interesting textures that can be interpreted in embroidery. The panel (bottom) by Wendy Pearman, based on a brick and flint wall, is worked in quilting and machine embroidery, with machine made lace between the flintstones to suggest cobwebs.

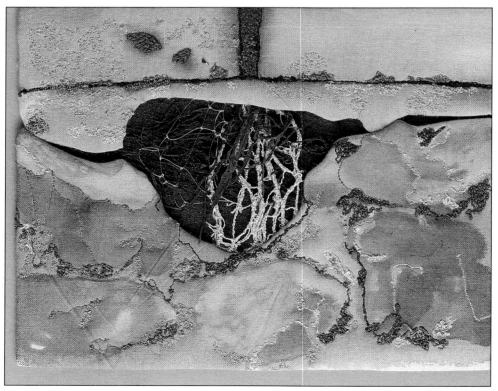

The delicate colours and textures of lichen on rock, sketched in a variety of coloured media (left) inspired this piece of machine embroidery (below). Fabric paints were sponged onto the coarse background fabric, and several sheer fabrics applied in places. Squiggly lines of machine embroidery in shiny threads express the richly detailed textures.

RUBBINGS   Another way of capturing textured surfaces — one that does not involve drawing — is to make rubbings. By examining as many different surfaces as possible, you will discover that some interesting patterns emerge when a wax crayon is rubbed over a sheet of paper placed on a rough surface.

It is best to use fairly thin paper, such as that used for typing, and the kind of wax crayons used by children. At brass-rubbing centres in Britain it is possible to buy special metallic rubbing crayons, which work very well on black paper; a rubbing produced in this way might serve as inspiration for a design worked in metallic threads on dark fabric. Either hold the fabric firmly or attach it with tape to the area to be rubbed; make the rubbing using the crayon on its side. It is fun to add other colours to the rubbing; these can be rubbed over each other to give definition in certain areas if a less uniform effect is required.

The rubbing pattern will then need to be transferred to the fabric by one of the methods described on pages 50–57. For an exact reproduction, the best method is to make the rubbing itself using fabric transfer crayons.

The illustrations here include a selection of rubbings from natural and man-made objects: frosted glass, a rough concrete wall, part of a wooden fence and a sea urchin shell. The shell has been interpreted in lines of couching and straight stitches over strips of sheer fabric. The frosted glass might be interpreted in buttonhole wheels. See what other patterns you can discover for possible use in embroidery.

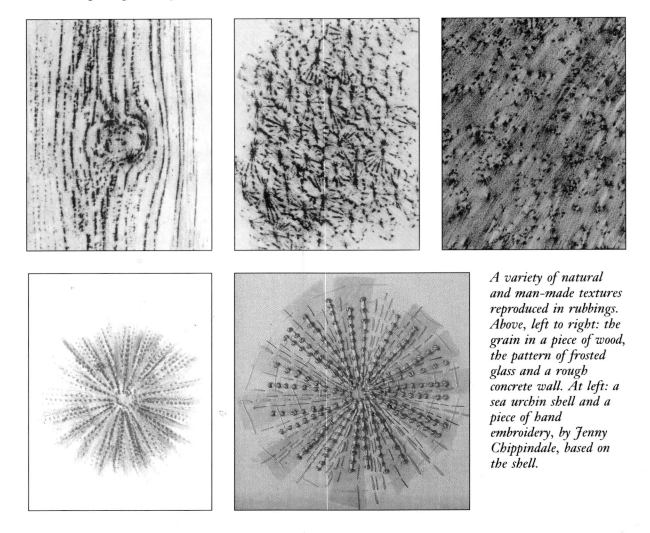

A variety of natural and man-made textures reproduced in rubbings. Above, left to right: the grain in a piece of wood, the pattern of frosted glass and a rough concrete wall. At left: a sea urchin shell and a piece of hand embroidery, by Jenny Chippindale, based on the shell.

MUSEUM STUDIES

Most museums have marvellous collections which will be of interest to the embroiderer. The list of items worth studying is endless, but you might start by looking at fossils, stuffed animals, and man-made artefacts such as pottery, jewellery and wood carvings.

Again, it is valuable to look closely and either photograph or draw the details that appeal to you. Once you have the information at home, you can develop this into your designs, selecting and enlarging parts of it if necessary. Most museums have a shop that sells postcards, but these are often much too small-scale to be useful, and you would do better to draw the patterns you like.

These three objects — a high relief carving of animals (above), a section of a fossil (above right) and part of a Roman mosaic floor — suggest some of the variety of design sources that can be found in museums.

Colour

We are surrounded by colour. So many different colours confront our eyes every day that we do not even consciously register most of them; and yet colour can significantly affect our mood and our well-being.

When you begin to study colour, even superficially, you discover how elusive and changeable it is. Without light there is no colour; for colour consists of light waves reflected off objects. In different lights, a colour changes. Moreover, the same colour may be perceived differently by different people; we never really know if we see exactly the same colour as someone else. Everyone tends to favour certain colours over others. Some people find reds and oranges exciting, while others find them hot and uncomfortable. Some people feel calm when surrounded by blue and green; others find these colours cold and depressing.

Whatever your own feelings about colour, you will find it a very important aspect of embroidery — one in which some experimentation will be worthwhile. To stick to tried and tested favourites would lead to some very dull and uninspiring work.

Impressionist and Post-Impressionist painters were masters of colour. They used it in highly

Opposite: two of the many paintings of Rouen Cathedral that Monet did at different times of day to show the varied colour effects produced in different kinds of light. Here the cathedral is shown in full afternoon sun (far left) and in more subdued light.

Right: 'Open Window at Collioure', by Matisse, illustrates this painter's use of intense, vibrant colours — a characteristic that earned him and others who painted in this way the nickname 'les Fauves' ('the wild beasts').

distinctive, revolutionary ways. The Impressionist approach was to apply pure colours in small, quick strokes, so that, at a short distance, they blend in the eye (known as optical mixing), producing a luminous, shimmering effect. Claude Monet, in particular, was fascinated by the way colours change in different light; and he sometimes painted a series of pictures of the same scene at different times of day and under different weather conditions, working on one canvas, then another, as the light changed. The Post-Impressionist Henri Matisse used bright colours in a more subjective way, juxtaposing them boldly so that they activate each other. The colours of a Matisse appear to have a life of their own.

In embroidery, too, a sensitive personal use of colour can be achieved by paying careful attention to the atmospheric quality of light, by looking closely at the subject matter and then by taking some degree of artistic licence.

To get some idea of how to use colour effectively, it may be helpful to begin by considering some of the basic principles of colour theory. By working through the exercises that follow, you will become familiar with how to combine and use the countless colours at your disposal.

THE COLOUR WHEEL

The basis of colour theory, as taught today, is the colour wheel. This consists, normally, of the twelve main colours of the spectrum, arranged in a circle. (Theoretically, it includes all the colours.) Three of these colours, red, yellow and blue, are called the primary colours, because they cannot be produced by mixing other colours. These can be combined to produce orange, green and violet, the secondary colours. These are, in turn, mixed with their nearest primaries to make the six tertiary colours. These colours, and all the other hues of the spectrum, are called pure colours, because they do not contain any black or white.

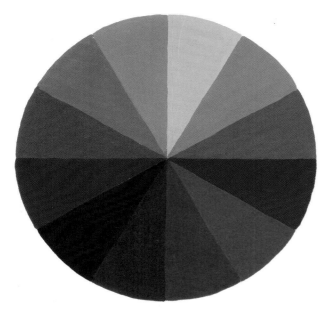

MIXING COLOURS   For these exercises you will need gouache paint in red, yellow, blue, black and white and several sheets of cartridge (drawing) or watercolour paper. Mark squares on the paper as done on these pages, then fill in the squares as instructed.

To mix secondary colours, begin with the three primary colours.

Mix red with yellow to make orange.
Mix yellow with blue to make green.
Mix red with blue to make violet.

You may find it difficult to obtain the exact secondary colours shown on the wheel (violet is especially elusive); this is because you are mixing pigments, not the pure light rays of the spectrum. For the following exercise, therefore, and for design work in colour, you may wish to add a purchased true violet and perhaps a green.

To mix tertiary colours, mix each secondary with its two adjacent primary colours. The resulting hues are:

red-orange
yellow-orange
yellow-green
blue-green
blue-violet
red-violet.

TINTS, TONES AND SHADES   In between the 12 basic colours of the wheel are many gradations of hue, some too subtle for the eye to perceive. And each of these colours can be made paler, duller or darker by the addition, respectively, of white, grey or black. The resulting colours are known as tints, tones and shades. The word 'shade' is commonly applied to any colour — as in 'a pale shade of pink' — but used correctly, it applies only to colours containing some black. Pink itself is a *tint* of red.

To discover some of the countless nuances possible in a single hue, fill in these three rows, of seven squares each, as described opposite.

Tints   Select one of your pure colours and paint it in the upper left-hand square as shown. Working across the row, gradually add white to your colour, using progressively less of the colour itself for each square. The right-hand square should contain almost all white, with just a trace of the original colour.

Tones   In the middle row, start with the pure colour in the left-hand square, then gradually add a mixture of white and black (grey) to your colour until, in the right-hand square, there is almost none of the colour left.

Shades   In the bottom row, start again with the pure colour in the left-hand square, then gradually add black in the same way as before.

You can see that with just one colour there is a great variety of possible tints, tones and shades. If you were to do this exercise with all the other hues of the colour spectrum, the range would be infinite.

Opposite: the colour wheel.

Above: mixing the primary colours to make the secondaries orange, green and violet (top row) and mixing the secondary colours to make the tertiaries.

Right: The addition of white, grey and black here produces tints, tones and shades of blue.

ANALOGOUS AND COMPLEMENTARY COLOURS

Although it is helpful to learn how to mix colours and to discover, through such exercises, how different colours react with each other, it is not necessary to use a scientific approach when using colours in embroidery. What we need to do, rather, is to develop an awareness of the colour schemes around us in nature and to learn to interpret them sensitively by choosing the most suitable threads and fabrics.

There is quite a long list of complex terminology associated with colour, but two words in particular are worth mentioning at this stage, as they are among the most useful.

ANALOGOUS refers to colours that are adjacent on the colour wheel. These are normally considered to be the colours that 'go' together, such as pinks and mauves, on one side of the colour wheel, and the greens and blues, on the other. Remember that tints, tones and shades of each colour are included.

Left: This piece of machine quilting uses a complementary colour scheme — red and green — including various tints and tones of these colours.

Opposite: The starting points for these two assortments of analogous colours were the complementary colours blue and orange. By collecting papers, fabrics and threads in the chosen colour and in those to either side of it, you can devise many interesting colour schemes.

COMPLEMENTARY colours are those that lie opposite each other on the colour wheel, such as green and red, orange and blue, violet and yellow. Again, the tints, tones, and shades of each colour are included, giving some extremely subtle complementary colours. In embroidery, complementaries can be effectively used by making a piece of work predominantly of one colour range and including a small amount of the complementary colour to give the work a 'lift'.

COLOUR EXERCISE 1: COMPLEMENTARY COLOURS

1. From magazine pages (see page 15), cut some strips of paper that are predominantly of one colour, including tints, tones and shades of that colour.
2. Glue these onto another sheet of paper, varying the width of each stripe by trimming or overlapping them.
3. Look at the colour wheel on page 38, and select the colour that is nearest to your magazine strips. Now find its complementary, located directly opposite on the colour wheel.
4. Cut several very narrow strips of paper in this complementary, and glue these over the original papers to see the effect of adding complementary colour to a piece of work. An example of a complementary colour scheme, represented with magazine paper strips, is shown on page 43.

COLOUR EXERCISE 2: ANALOGOUS COLOURS

1. Look at the colour scheme that you have just made. Choosing first the predominant colour, collect scraps of magazine paper in tints, tones and shades of that colour and the colours that are adjacent to it on the colour wheel. If your collection of thread and fabrics is extensive enough, select those in the appropriate colours, and explore the possibilities of using them together in a piece of embroidery.
2. Now do the same thing with the complementary colour. Arrange the two groups of papers, threads and fabrics in different piles. You may be surprised at some of the unlikely — yet successful — colour combinations you achieve.

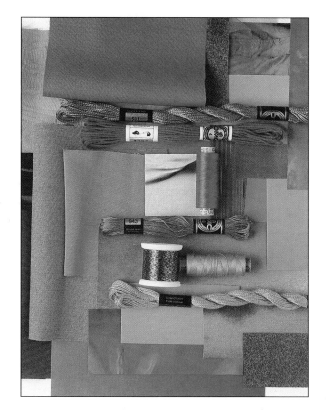

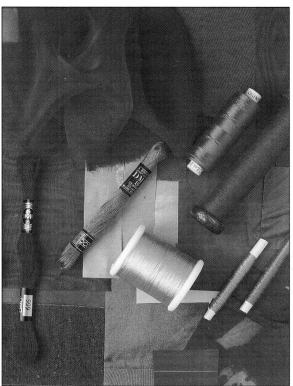

LOOKING AT COLOUR SCHEMES

There are many lovely colour schemes around us in our environment, ready for us to use as they are, or with only slight alterations. Many totally different subjects have similar colour schemes; for example, compare the picture of rusting chicken wire and the one showing paint peeling off an old door.

To derive a colour scheme from a photograph, look carefully at it to see how much of each colour it contains. These proportions of colour will vary from one part of the photograph to another, providing you with several options in devising a colour scheme for the embroidery.

Using a photograph of your choice, and magazine papers, as in the previous exercises, construct one or more colour schemes, like the one shown opposite. Try to keep the proportions the same as those in the photograph as a whole and those in different parts of it. Then try adjusting the proportions slightly to see what different effects you can create.

A further valuable exercise is to interpret a colour scheme in thread windings. These are very useful for future reference, especially if you attach details of the threads used to the back of each sample. To make one, first cover a piece of cardboard with double-sided tape, then peel away the paper backing of the tape as the thread-winding progresses.

These photographs suggested the colour scheme for the exercise at right. Magazine papers and a thread winding were used to represent the chosen proportions (from the paintwork), used as the basis for the stitchery.

DRAWING *and* PAINTING

lthough it is possible to produce attractive designs for embroidery from tracings, rubbings and cut paper shapes, the most satisfactory approach, if you are designing a decorative panel, or picture, is to make a drawing or painting of your chosen subject. In this way, you become intimately acquainted with the subject, and the resulting embroidery is more truly your own original work. A camera simply records information; whereas your eye is selective; it focuses, physically and psychologically, on the elements of a subject that are important to you, screening out irrelevant details. No two people will see or interpret a subject in the same way.

Many people are frightened of drawing, and insist that they lack the ability; but this is because they give up too easily or set too high standards for themselves. There is no need to produce a finished work of art, suitable for framing; all you are aiming for is a drawing that will serve as a basis for interpretation in embroidery. The very act of drawing will force you to look closely at the subject — much more closely than if you were tracing from a photograph — and will reveal aspects of its form, texture and colour that will suggest suitable techniques and materials for the embroidery itself.

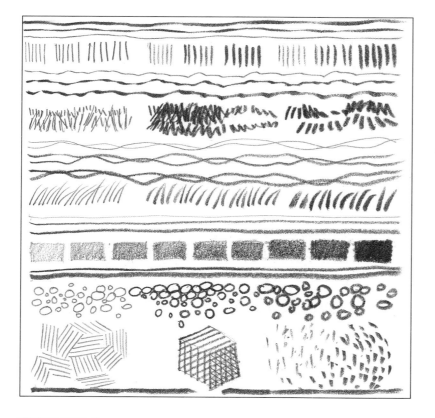

Left: A soft pencil was used for these drawing exercises, which illustrate some of the range of effects that can be obtained using only one medium. Note especially the tonal contrasts, from light, thin lines to bold, heavy ones. Try making similar marks with pencils, crayons and pastels.

DRAWING EXERCISES

Begin by familiarizing yourself with the various drawing media available (see page 15). You will find some easier to control than others; but it is well worthwhile learning to use as many as possible, so that you will have a large repertoire of different effects, appropriate to different subject matter. Use these media on different kinds of paper, from smooth to highly textured, to see how they vary from one background to another. Try tinted papers, as well as white, for different levels of contrast.

With each drawing medium, practise making as many different marks as you can think of: try short, straight parallel lines, varying the pressure to make them lighter and darker, then varying the spacing to produce interesting rhythms; draw

Right: These fuchsias are a good subject for embroidery and also for drawing exercises. The blossoms have a sculptural quality and gracefully curving lines, and the leaves have strong, simple shapes.

Pages 46 and 47: sketches in a variety of drawing and painting media, based on the fuchsias. Note how some of the sketches emphasize the linear qualities of the flowers; others, the contrast of tonal values.

little clumps of lines, with the clumps at different angles, or superimposed to produce cross hatching; draw wavy lines to suggest water ripples and gracefully bending ones to suggest grasses blowing in the wind; draw circles to suggest pebbles or bunches of grapes; using a soft medium, cover an area with dots or small smudges to produce a stippled effect; vary the density of the stippling to suggest shading; apply dots of different colours to produce effects similar to Impressionist or Pointillist painting. See how many different tones you can achieve using, for example, a 4B pencil; draw ten squares on the paper, then fill them with progressively darker tones. Such exercises will help you acquire confidence in handling the different drawing media.

MAKING A SKETCH   When choosing a subject to sketch (and possibly interpret in embroidery), resist the temptation to begin by drawing the whole thing in all its complexity. Instead, begin by drawing some of its component parts, so that you become thoroughly familiar with its details. Then you can apply your visual understanding to a drawing of the whole subject.

Train yourself to look really closely at every part of whatever you are drawing. Look, for example, at one of the fuchsia blossoms in the photograph on page 45. Examine the way the petals curve upwards; compare the length of the stamens to the length of the blossom as a whole; notice the angle formed by the leaf veins.

Of course, your drawing should not be laboured, or even finished-looking. You don't want to include every detail; instead, emphasize those you consider most important. Concentrate on the main lines and shapes and how they relate to each other. You may also sometimes find it helpful to draw the negative shapes. The different textures and colours can be suggested by the techniques shown opposite and by a skilful use of coloured media. You may find that you need to combine two or more different media in the final drawing, in order to convey the variety of line and texture that you envisage for the embroidery. Even though the drawing is simply a means to an end, a little time spent developing the image on paper will pay dividends when you come to interpret it in fabric, thread and stitches.

PAINTING EXERCISES

Liquid media are somewhat more difficult to control than dry ones, but they can produce wonderful effects. To begin with, buy yourself some gouache, watercolours and/or inks in several colours, and spend some time just playing with them and becoming familiar with their characteristics. Work on fairly thick cartridge (drawing) paper, using several different sizes of brush and applying them in different ways — using just the tip of the brush, for example, then dragging it flat over the paper. Try diluting the paint to a thin wash; also use it fairly thick, on the point of a dry brush. Working on wet paper will often produce effects that can be simulated in fabric paints. Practise making all sorts of different lines and dots, as you did with the dry drawing media.

Try applying the paint with different implements, such as bits of sponge, or even your finger. An interesting negative image can be created by first drawing on the paper with an ordinary household candle and then applying coloured ink or watercolour to the whole area. The wax acts as a resist, leaving an image of white lines on the paper where the paint is not absorbed. White lines can also be created on a previously painted background by means of ordinary bleach, applied with a mapping pen.

When you have gained some facility in handling paints, try using them to produce a design for a small piece of stitchery. Later, you can use your paintings for more ambitious embroideries.

Some of the many different effects that can be achieved with paints – in this case, watercolours. Among them: brickwork suggested by a flat, chisel-shaped brush; delicate flowers made by rotating the brush; vertical strokes of full-strength colours blended on the paper; a leaf drawn with the tip of the brush over a wet wash; an orange wash blotted with a rag; wax crayon resist and wash suggesting a starry sky; foliage depicted with sponged-on paint and heightened with paint applied on the point of a chisel-shaped brush; a negative shape outlined with grey wash, then given a vitreous texture with a few strokes of beige and grey; green and brown strokes superimposed to suggest a field of grasses.

From DESIGN *to* EMBROIDERY

To get from the design stage to the embroidery itself can be a difficult transition. Fabric is considerably more expensive than paper, and a blank piece of fabric can appear very daunting. Fortunately, however, there are a number of different ways of getting the design onto the fabric, and once you become familiar with these methods you will find this transition stage much easier.

Two traditional methods are described on pages 56–57. Both of these involve transferring outlines to the fabric; and they are very useful if you require an accurate reproduction of the original drawing or tracing.

However, if you enjoyed the experience of drawing and painting on paper, you may also enjoy painting the design onto the fabric using one of the fabric paints available. These methods are a logical step from painting and drawing on paper, and they provide a far less intimidating surface on which to work than a plain fabric. They also have the advantage of giving additional depth to the work; the textured stitching seems to emerge naturally from the background, rather than merely sitting on it.

The various kinds of fabric paint are described on pages 18–19. In the following pages I shall illustrate their use.

Above: These variegated grapes lent themselves to interpretation in fabric paints and stitchery.

Left: A cork is used to print the grape images onto the fabric. The vine leaves themselves were dipped into the paint and used for printing the leaves.

Right: Seeding stitches are here being worked on the background to build up texture and accentuate certain areas.

FABRIC PAINTS

These products — also called 'permanent' fabric paints — are widely available and easy to use. They are applied directly to the fabric with a brush, sponge or other implement. They can be diluted with water and mixed together to obtain the desired shade and consistency. Practise making random marks on a piece of spare fabric before you attempt to paint the design itself.

1. Attach the fabric (previously washed, to remove any finish, and ironed) to a board or other flat surface with drawing pins (thumbtacks) or masking tape.
2. Pour a little of each colour into a saucer or the separate compartments of a palette. Add water, if necessary, to achieve the right consistency.
3. Apply the main shapes of your design with a brush, sponge or other implement.
4. When the paint has dried thoroughly, place the fabric face down on the ironing board, which has first been covered with a cloth; place another cloth on top to protect the iron, and iron the fabric at the temperature recommended by the manufacturer for that fabric. The colour is now permanently fixed and will withstand washing.

In some cases you may wish to apply the paint in two or more stages: blocking in the background with fairly dilute paint, allowing this to dry, and then painting on more defined shapes with a fine brush. For a well-defined image, a stencil can be used. Sprayed and speckled effects can be achieved by means of a mouth diffuser or by running a piece of cardboard over a toothbrush (draw the cardboard towards you).

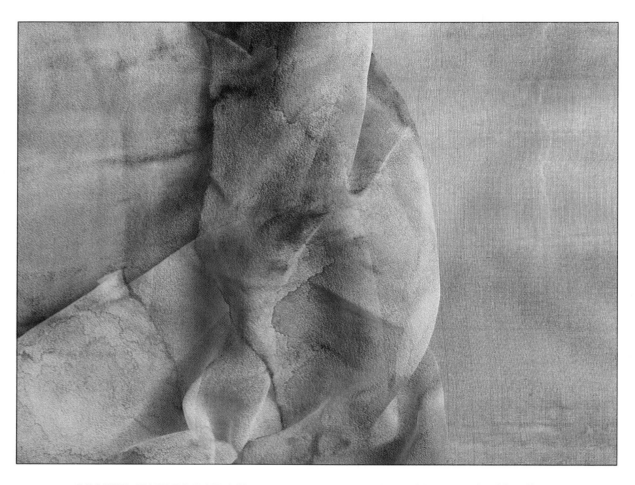

LIQUID FABRIC PAINTS

These lovely paints are intended especially for silk, but they give good results on other fabrics also. As the name implies, they have a very fluid consistency and will run freely over the fabric unless prevented from doing so by means of a resist, applied before painting. Their runny quality, however, can be exploited to create beautiful multicoloured fabrics, which can be used not only for embroidery — especially free machine work and quilting — but also for patchwork.

You will need to do some experimenting on various fabrics to get the feel of these paints and learn how to control them; but your patience will be well rewarded, and you may produce some happy accidents with your first attempts. Begin by painting some broad stripes across the fabric, letting the colours run into each other; then go on to create more complex patterns.

1. Stretch the fabric (preferably silk) onto a rectangular frame so that it is taut; this will help to prevent puddles from forming. (Strips of double-sided tape on the frame will make it easy to attach the fabric.) If, however, a marbled effect is desired, the fabric can simply be laid onto a sheet of plastic; this will provide a gently irregular surface.

2. Apply the paint to the fabric in your chosen design, using a brush or sponge. For a more diluted effect, add a little water to the paint, or first dampen the fabric with a sponge. For a textured quality, sprinkle sea salt onto the fabric while the paint is still wet.

3. When the paint is dry, iron the fabric on the wrong side (with a cloth above and below for protection) to fix the colours, using the manufacturer's recommended temperature. If salt has been used, wash the fabric after ironing to remove it.

USING A RESIST   This glue-like liquid is available in a clear form, which washes out, and in several colours, including black, gold and silver, which leave outlines in those colours on the fabric. It is available where liquid fabric paints are sold.

1. Stretch the fabric onto a frame so that it is taut.
2. Draw the outlines on the fabric with the resist, using either the plastic nozzle provided or a fine brush. Allow the resist to dry.
3. Apply the paints within the outlines. Subtle effects can be produced by applying two or more colours within an area and allowing them to run together.
4. Fix the colours by ironing in the usual way.

Opposite: Subtle gradations of colour can be achieved with liquid fabric paints, as shown here on silk chiffon and on some opaque silk. The mottled effects were produced by sprinkling sea salt on the still-wet fabric.

Above: Colourless and gold resists were used for the outlines of this rectangular design before liquid paints were applied.

Right: a floral design delineated in resist and coloured with liquid fabric paints.

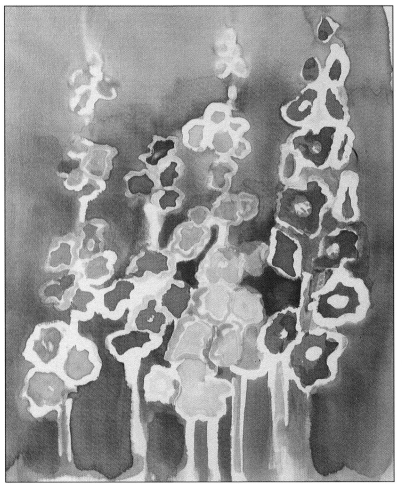

FABRIC MARKERS

Similar to fibre tip pens, these markers are specifically designed for drawing on fabrics. They are probably most effective when used on wet fabric, but they can also be used for adding details to a piece of dry, painted fabric.

1. Stretch the fabric onto a rectangular frame and spray it with water; this gives a softer outline.
2. Draw the design with the felt markers, overlaying the colours, if you wish, to mix them. If more details are desired, allow the fabric to dry before adding them.
3. Fix the colours by ironing in the usual way. The fabric is completely washable.

TRANSFER PAINTS

If you are reluctant to paint a design directly onto the fabric, transfer paints are a good alternative. In this method, you first paint the design onto paper, then iron it off onto the fabric. If the first design is not satisfactory, you can correct it on another sheet of paper before transferring it.

There are, however, two important points to remember about these paints. The image will be reversed on the fabric; so you must either draw it the wrong way round on the paper or do a preliminary drawing, trace it onto some tracing paper and then turn this over and paint on the other side.

The other point to remember is that the colours vary considerably according to the fabric

These delphiniums (above) served as the inspiration for a design using transfer paints. The painted image (near right) on paper, shown after ironing, is reversed on the fabric (far right) and fainter.

used; on synthetics (for which they are best suited) they are fairly intense, but on cotton and silk they are very subtle. They are always paler on the fabric than on the paper. Before transferring the design itself, always make a test print of the colours on spare fabric. The same design can be printed more than once, but subsequent prints will be paler than the first.

It is often a good idea to apply the main design with transfer paints, then use ordinary fabric paint on top of the image to add details or to soften the outlines. This will make the design less representational and give it a freer quality.

1. Draw the design on thin cartridge (drawing) paper, remembering that it will be reversed on the fabric.

2. Colour the design with the transfer paints, diluting them if necessary.
3. When the paint is dry, place the design right side up on the fabric (first protecting the board with a cloth), and press it for at least 10 seconds, with the iron as hot as the fabric will allow. Move the iron very gently so as not to blur the image. Lift a corner cautiously to make sure the image is transferred; if necessary, apply the iron again.

TRANSFER CRAYONS

Like transfer paints, these are used by drawing onto a piece of paper, then ironing the design onto fabric. They, too, work better on fabrics containing at least some synthetic fibres. These crayons are particularly useful for making rubbings, which can be ironed onto fabric to give instant designs suitable for stitching or quilting.

Some experimenting with the colours is advisable, as they tend to be rather bright. It may be necessary to go over the whole design with the black crayon to make the colours more subtle.

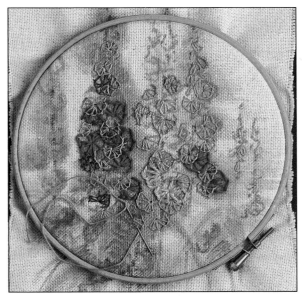

This interpretation (above) of the delphiniums was applied directly to the fabric with fabric markers. Buttonhole wheels are being worked over the blooms.

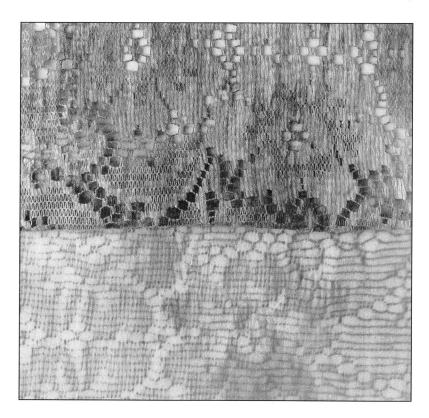

Left: Both of these effects were made with transfer crayons. A rubbing was made of cream coloured lace curtain fabric and then ironed onto voile (below). Then the same colours — blue, green and violet — were crayonned onto paper and ironed onto the lace fabric (top).

Opposite, above: a tacked design with the tissue tracing partially torn away.

Opposite, below: the prick-and-pounce method, showing the original subject matter, the tracing with holes pricked in it and the dotted-line image, in the process of being fixed with water-erasable pen.

1. Make a rubbing using fabric transfer crayons on thin paper, such as lightweight cartridge (drawing) paper. Or draw an original design (remember that it will be reversed on the fabric).
2. Iron off the rubbing onto a fabric that contains some synthetic fibres, such as polyester-cotton. Use a cloth on the ironing board to protect it.

TRADITIONAL DESIGN TRANSFER METHODS

These two methods are excellent ways of accurately reproducing the outlines of a design previously drawn or traced on paper. The 'prick and pounce' method is especially well suited to highly detailed designs; the tissue method is ideal for positioning the main lines of a simpler design, on which the stitchery can be worked freely.

PRICK AND POUNCE This is an extremely old method of transferring a design onto fabric, but as it is one of the most accurate, it is still used today.

1. Trace the design onto firm tracing paper. Place the traced design wrong side up on a turkish towel, blanket or other soft surface. (By pricking from the wrong side, you ensure that the smooth side of the paper — and not the rough marks produced where the needle emerges — will be in contact with the fabric; this helps to produce neat dots.)
2. Insert the blunt end of a thick, sharp needle into a cork to make a pricker. Using this, pierce holes along all the design lines. The holes need to be close together for intricate parts of the design, but can be farther apart for less detailed areas.
3. Place the pricked tracing right side up on the fabric and pin it securely in place. Rub the pounce powder — powdered chalk or talcum powder — through the holes, using either a pad made from a roll of soft fabric, such as felt, or a piece of cotton wool (absorbent cotton). For light fabrics a little powdered charcoal needs to be added to the chalk.

4. Carefully remove the tracing. The design will appear on the fabric as a series of dots. Join these up quickly before the powder gets blown away, using a water-erasable pen. If the project will entail much time-consuming hand stitchery, it is best to use some watercolour paint, slightly darker than the fabric, applied with a fine sable brush. This will be permanent enough to work the embroidery but not so obtrusive as to show after the embroidery is worked.

TACKING (BASTING) THROUGH TISSUE   This is another accurate method of transferring designs. It is particularly suitable for highly textured fabrics such as velvet or slubbed silk.

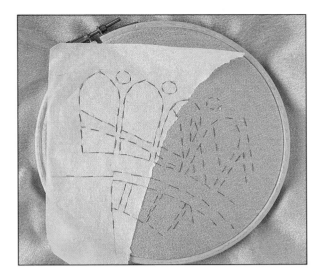

1. Trace the design onto tissue paper.
2. Pin the tissue to the fabric (previously framed up), and using a single strand of fine sewing thread, work running stitches along the lines of the design.
3. When the whole design has been transferred, carefully tear away the tissue paper, leaving

the design outlines on the fabric. This can most easily be done if you first gently run the point of a needle along the stitched lines. Remove the running stitches as you work the embroidery — preferably a little ahead of the stitching.

STITCHERY

For most people the word 'embroidery' immediately conjures up an image of stitchery worked on a piece of fabric. Certainly stitches are one of the oldest ways of decorating fabric, and they feature prominently in textiles produced by ancient cultures all over the world.

Although the styles of embroidery developed by different peoples vary considerably, certain stitches are common to widely separated countries. Not surprisingly, these are generally the simplest stitches — those that people would quickly discover for themselves. For example, running stitch (often used for pattern darning) and cross stitch appear in the embroideries of many far-flung cultures, including those of Russia, Italy and the Scandinavian countries. Other stitches, such as Cretan, Roumanian and Portu-

Left: This detail from a typically fanciful piece of English crewel work (circa 1700) shows a variety of stitches, including satin stitch, long and short stitch (the shaded areas) and Vandyke stitch.

Opposite: Counted thread stitchery is typical of many countries. This example, a coffin cloth from Telemark, Norway, includes cross stitch and other counted-thread stitches, worked in wool and silk on linen.

guese knot, are associated with a particular country, where they are believed to have originated. Through migration, trade and travel, embroidery stitches have become more and more widespread, so that today the embroiderer has literally hundreds of stitches from which to choose.

Some of these stitches are extremely complex and have limited use, because their appeal depends on their being worked very precisely, not on any representational or expressive quality. Conversely, some of the simpler stitches, such as cross, running, chain and satin stitch — are among the most useful, because they can be worked in so many ways to achieve such diverse effects.

It is not necessary to be able to work vast numbers of different stitches; many of the best embroiderers working today restrict their reper-toire to only a few. The beginner, too, should first master the basic techniques of a few stitches and then explore the possibilities of using them in a creative way. All you need is this basic vocabulary of stitches and a sense of adventure to be able to use them effectively.

In order to get you started, I suggest that you look at the effects of taking two simple stitches and altering them by varying their direction, shape and size. These exercises should be worked in an experimental way, without giving any thought to what the finished result will be.

Next, we shall look at how to achieve specific effects with a few different stitches. In particular, we shall be noting that some stitches are more suitable for making lines, others for areas of texture and still others for filling in areas of a pattern.

Left: This exercise in hand stitching, by Fay Twydell, is based on a rhubarb stem and includes stem stitch, couching and French knots.

It will soon be noted, however, that such categories are not rigid and that most stitches can be used for different purposes. Lines of chain stitch, for example, can be massed together and superimposed to create richly textured areas.

It is a good idea to work through these exercises systematically, in order to achieve a certain level of skill in selecting and using the appropriate threads, before embarking on a project.

Right: Seeding and lines of chain stitch provide an interesting contrast of textures in this embroidery, by Angela Howard, based on a peony stem.

Below: Freely worked encroaching straight stitches, using a variety of threads, have been used by Kay Swancutt to suggest a summer meadow.

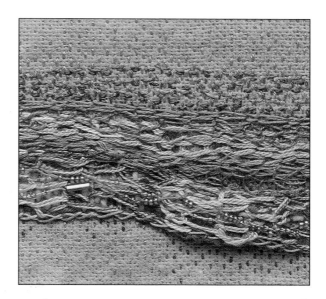

FLY STITCH

This simple stitch consists basically of an open loop held down by a vertical stitch, forming a 'Y' shape. It is one of the most useful stitches.

WORKING THE STITCH IN THE TRADITIONAL MANNER Bring the needle up at the upper left-hand corner of the 'Y'. Keeping the thread under the needle, to form a loop, insert the needle at the upper right-hand corner and bring it out at the centre of the 'Y', as shown. Take it down to form the tail of the 'Y', and bring it up in the position for the next stitch.

Work three or four stitches to get the feel and rhythm of the stitch.

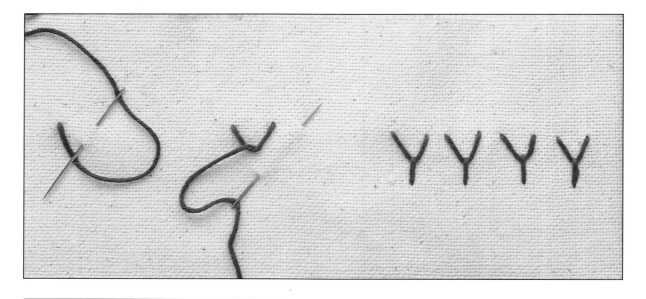

ALTERING THE SHAPE OF THE STITCH When you have mastered the basic stitch, try altering the shape of the stiches, making them short and fat, then long and thin.

Because it is made in two movements, fly stitch is extremely flexible. The length of the tail can be altered, as well as the shape of the body of the stitch.

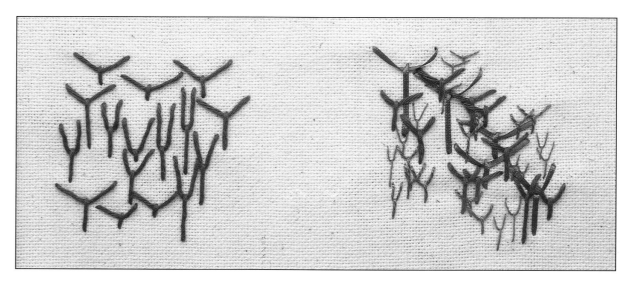

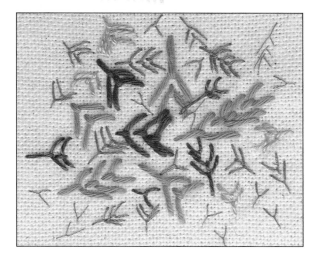

USING DIFFERENT THREADS It is possible to make the stitches different from one another by varying the type of thread used. Try the same exercise as above, but this time use some thick threads, such as knitting yarns, ribbons and strips of fabric, as well as thinner threads such a coton à broder, silks and crewel wool.

VARYING THE DIRECTION So far, all the stitches have been worked vertically. They can also be worked in curves and circles and in horizontal, vertical and diagonal lines — in fact, in any direction — to suit the subject matter.

NOTE that for clarity the stitches in these pages are shown as if worked in the hand. If worked in a frame, they would entail using the needle vertically.

Right: This small piece of stitchery, inspired by rosebay willowherb, is worked entirely in fly stitch, using several different threads, elongating some of the stitches and inverting others.

BUTTONHOLE STITCH

Buttonhole is one of the most familiar of all stitches. It is sometimes used, worked widely spaced, on the edges of blankets — hence its other name, blanket stitch. Small, closely worked buttonhole stitches are used on the edges and bars of cutwork embroidery. Like fly stitch, buttonhole consists basically of a loop, but in this case each loop is held in place by the next stitch.

WORKING THE STITCH IN THE TRADITIONAL MANNER Begin by working the stitch in a horizontal line, from left to right. Bring the needle up on the line (first marked on the fabric if you like). Take it down a short distance to the right, above the line, and bring it up directly below, keeping the loop under the needle. Pull the thread through, and move the needle to the right to form the next stitch. Continue, forming a row of evenly worked stitches.

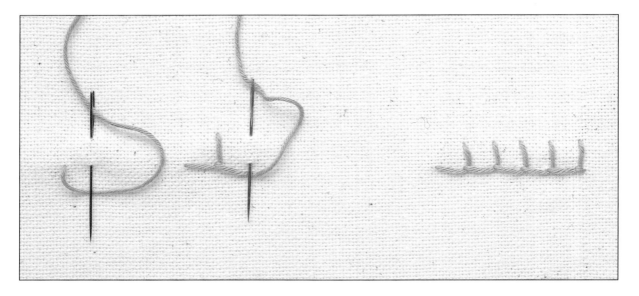

Right: stages in working detached buttonhole stitch, along with some massed shapes of detached buttonhole worked in different threads.

Opposite: Various forms of buttonhole stitch, including regularly worked, overlapping rows and some detached buttonhole, have been used to suggest rock formations.

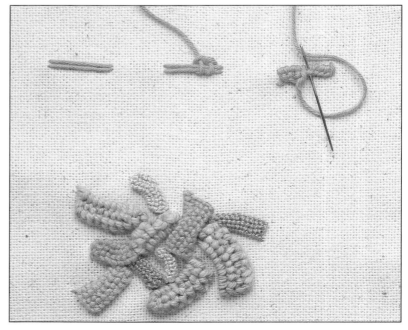

ALTERING THE SHAPE AND DIRECTION Keeping the vertical stitches upright, alter the spaces between them, and also vary the length, so altering the angle of the horizontal lines.

Next, try inverting the rows, so that some of the stitches point downwards. Superimpose the rows, and see what different effects are created by different threads.

BUTTONHOLE WHEELS Work the stitch in circles, radiating around a central point. Portions of wheels will prevent the effect from looking mechanical, as will varying the spacing of the stitches and varying their length, which produces a spiky effect. Wheels can also be worked with the

bars at the centre, producing a star-like pattern, as can be seen in the sample on page 68.

DETACHED BUTTONHOLE STITCH Buttonhole stitch can also be worked independently of the fabric, over a foundation bar of threads. To make the bar, take the needle back and forth two or three times across the required length. Cover the bar with buttonhole stitches, without taking the needle through the fabric. For subsequent rows, work into the stitches of the previous row. For a scallop shape, work one stitch less in each row. Try working a number of pieces of detached buttonhole, varying the thread and the direction as shown. The pieces can be overlapped to form a dense texture.

THE EFFECTS OF STITCHERY

It has already been shown that stitches look much more interesting if they are worked in a free way. However, some serious thought must be given to their use, as completely random stitchery can look very untidy. The embroiderer needs to acquire a sensitive approach to the threads and fabrics being used. The stitches should not look as if they are just added to the background, but, rather, as if they belong to the fabric and actually grow out of it. The resulting piece of stitchery should be a textile in its own right — not just a piece of fabric that has been decorated.

The use of fabric paints can help to achieve a subtle effect, because they form a link between the fabric and the stitch in terms of colour. The use of different threads will also help: thin threads will sink into the fabric, whereas thicker ones will give a more textured effect by projecting from the surface. As the stitch exercises on the previous pages have demonstrated, even more texture can be achieved by working stitches one on top of another.

Every embroidery stitch has its own character; and some — as we have seen in the case of fly and buttonhole stitch — have more than one. Nevertheless, different stitches often share a common characteristic and so can be grouped into 'families'. Not every embroiderer, or every writer on the subject, classifies stitches in the same way; but I find it useful to think of stitches in terms of their potential for suggesting areas of line, texture or pattern.

LINEAR STITCHES   These stitches, however they are worked, will give a linear movement. They include chain stitch, couching, backstitch and stem stitch. Fly stitch has a linear quality, but when thickly massed is good for suggesting texture, such as that of grasses.

TEXTURAL STITCHES   Although all stitches add texture to the fabric, some of them are especially well suited to represent the texture of natural or man-made objects. They include buttonhole stitch (especially wheels and pieces of detached buttonhole), French knots, bullion knots and velvet stitch (cut and uncut).

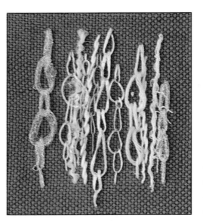

Linear stitches: chain stitch, stem stitch and couching.

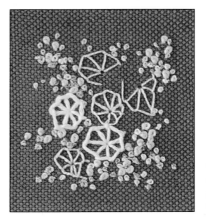

Textural stitches: French knots and buttonhole wheels.

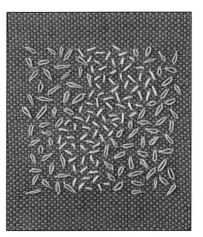

Pattern stitches: detached chain and seeding.

PATTERN STITCHES   These stitches are particularly useful for filling in areas of pattern in a design, or for making patterns by the shape of the stitch itself. They include cross stitch, detached chain, seeding and eyelets. Effects of shading can be produced by varying the density of the stitches.

LINEAR STITCHES

Linear stitches are important in giving a sense of movement and rhythm to a piece of embroidery. They can achieve different effects by the direction in which they are used. Vertical lines tend to suggest a thrusting, upward movement, as in the growth of plants in early spring. Horizontal lines give a feeling of calm and repose, which can be employed effectively in seascapes and in landscapes featuring farmland, for example. The shape of the lines is important: curved lines can suggest undulating waves or rolling hills; straight lines have a harder, spiky feeling, reminiscent of icicles or streaks of lighting. The spacing of lines also needs careful consideration. They will look best if some are grouped close together and others spaced farther apart. The use of different threads, such as knitting yarns, ribbons and strips of fabric, as well as fine embroidery threads, can all help to give the work the necessary variety and textural interest.

RUNNING STITCH is the simplest of all stitches. However by alternating the length and spacing of the stitches on adjacent rows, many subtle effects can be achieved.

BACKSTITCH creates a thin, solid line. It can be made more interesting by varying the length of the stitches and by working it in different threads.

STEM STITCH has an attractive rope-like quality and is especially useful, as its name implies, for representing stems. The line can be made thicker by working the stitches at an angle to the line.

CHAIN STITCH is an extremely versatile stitch with numerous variations. Try altering the size of the loops, as shown.

COUCHING   This stitch is used for applying thick threads to the surface of the fabric. The thread used for couching the main thread to the fabric is normally fine, and the stitches as inconspicuous as possible. However fascinating effects can be produced by using a thicker thread and conspicuous stitches; note particularly the buttonhole stitches used to couch the strip of fabric at the bottom of the sample below.

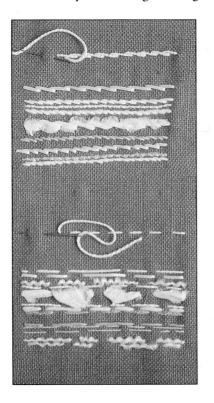
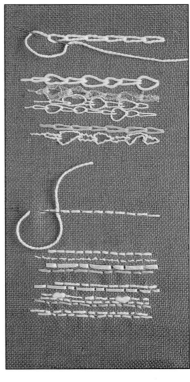
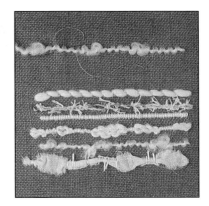

Far left: stem stitch (top) and running stitch.

Left: chain stitch and backstitch.

Above: couching.

TEXTURAL STITCHES

These stitches are ideal for interpreting textured surfaces in embroidery. Interesting textures can be found in many natural objects, such as the ridged surface of bark, the strata of rock formations or moss growing on a wall, and also in man-made objects, such as bricks or tiled roofs. Stitchery is the perfect medium in which to explore these qualities and to experiment with some of the wonderfully varied threads in your work basket.

Many different stitches can be used for suggesting texture; some will become three-dimensional by being overlapped and built up in layers. Here I have shown four different textural stitches, to be tried with a variety of threads.

BUTTONHOLE WHEELS naturally suggest masses of blossoms; they can also be used for certain kinds of rock formations and coral.

FRENCH KNOTS are among the most appealing of all stitches, with a delightfully tactile quality. For best results, wrap the thread only once around the needle. For different-sized knots, use different thicknesses of thread.

BULLION KNOTS are similar to French knots, with a slightly directional quality. The effect is well worth the practice they require. Bring the thread to the surface, and take the needle down a short distance away. Bring it up where the thread emerges, and wind the thread several times around the needle. Pull the thread through the loops, and take the needle down again where it was inserted.

VELVET STITCH derives its name from the fuzzy effect that results if the loops are cut. Leaving the loops uncut, as shown, produces a more varied texture. Work the stitches starting at the bottom and moving upward. First make a loop from lower left to upper right. Bring the needle out where it emerged, and, holding the loop in place, work a vertical stitch from upper right to lower right. Pull the thread flat, then insert the needle at upper left to complete the cross stitch which holds the loop in place.

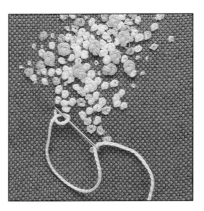

French knots; note that the thread is taken once around the needle.

Buttonhole wheels, including some partial wheels.

Velvet stitch, with the loops left uncut.

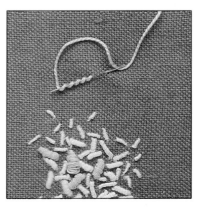

Bullion knots.

PATTERN STITCHES

These are essentially all-over stitches, which can be used to fill areas of pattern, as in traditional cross stitch and Assisi work. They can also be used where a design has a large area of background which needs some discreet stitchery in matching threads to blend in with the main stitchery of the design. Still another function of pattern stitches is to link areas together to lead the eye from one part of the design to another.

SEEDING consists merely of small, individual straight stitches worked in all directions. Try varying the spacing of the stitch to suggest shading or modelling.

DETACHED CHAIN is essentially the same as linear chain stitch, but each loop is held in place by a small stitch worked as shown.

CROSS STITCH can be worked in the traditional manner, as shown, or more freely, for an irregular appearance.

EYELETS are useful for stylized, flat floral areas. Open the centre hole slightly with the needle, and always take the needle down into the hole, not up.

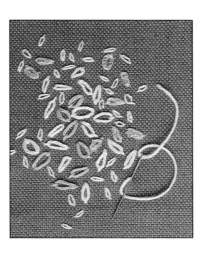

Detached chain stitches.

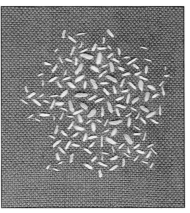

Seeding stitches.

Eyelets (far left) and cross stitches (left) are more interesting when worked irregularly, as shown.

PROJECT USING LINEAR STITCHES

Once you have mastered a few linear stitches, it is a good idea to employ one or two of them in a small piece of work, so that you can begin to get a feeling for their expressive potential. Choose a subject with an intrinsically linear quality. It might be something quite simple, such as some rushes growing at the edge of a pond or cloud patterns in the sky; or you might like to try something slightly more complex, such as these graceful fuchsia blossoms which are based on the photograph on page 45.

To provide a framework and background for the stitchery, apply the basic shape(s) to the fabric with fabric paints. I have painted the fuchsia blossoms and leaves onto the fabric using a brush; for the background I used a sponge. The sample should be fairly small, so I would suggest using fine threads. The ones chosen for this sample are perlé cotton, coton à broder, soft embroidery cotton and crewel wool.

Don't try to incorporate too many stitches in the work; otherwise it can look untidy. I used chain stitch and stem stitch, for a contrast of thickness. If your shapes are more solid, you may wish to couch some thick threads onto the work.

It is important to choose a focal area, or one part of the sample which is to be more prominent than the rest. This will need to be worked more densely, possibly with thicker threads, so that it contrasts with smooth, less densely worked areas. One advantage of the painted background is that it does not have to be entirely covered with stitchery. The unstitched parts of the design will complement and set off the stitched areas.

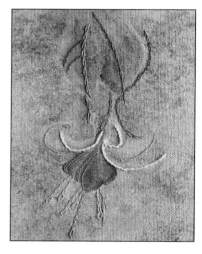

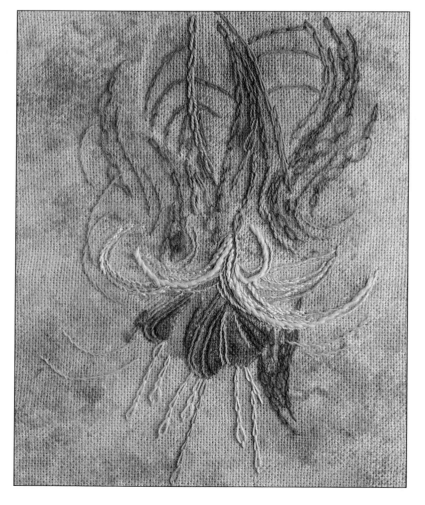

This little embroidery is based on the photograph shown on page 45. The image was first applied with fabric paints, then the dominant lines were established (above) using the two chosen stitches, chain and stem. In the completed embroidery (right) the shapes are further enhanced with more lines of stitching which contrast effectively with the sponged, painted background.

PROJECT USING TEXTURAL STITCHES

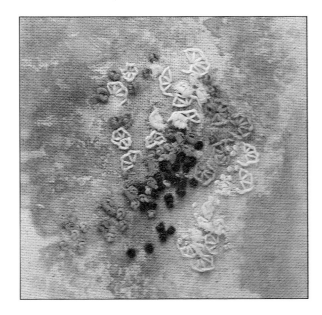

Now try a sample piece of stitchery suggesting texture. Select a subject with strong textural appeal, such as a crumbling stone wall or a bit of shoreline strewn with pebbles, shells and seaweed. The design shown here was inspired by a photograph of lichen on a rock in Cornwall. Here I used transfer paints to provide a background for the stitchery. In this case I simply sponged some paints in suitable colours onto the paper and transferred the colours onto a piece of furnishing fabric. The threads used for the embroidery were crewel wool, perlé cotton, soft (matte) embroidery cotton, thick knitting yarn and knitting tape. The stitches chosen are French knots, buttonhole wheels – including partially worked wheels – and detached buttonhole bars.

An early stage of this embroidery, inspired by lichen on a rock, shows the texture beginning to 'emerge' from the painted background, in the form of buttonhole wheels and French knots. In the completed work, a dense texture has been built up, with the addition of more wheels and knots, as well as bits of detached buttonhole.

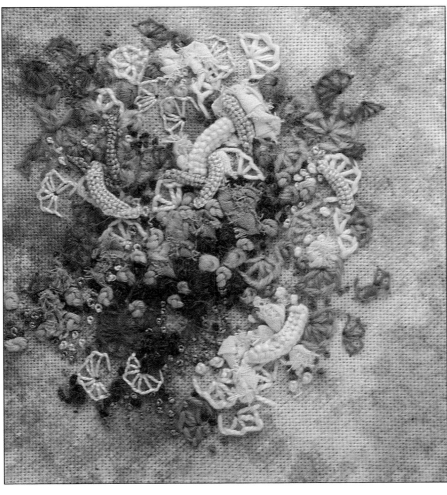

PROJECT USING PATTERN STITCHES

So far, we have looked at stitches that can be used to indicate natural forms. By the nature of the lines that they made, stem stitch and chain stitch conveyed the graceful curves of fuchsia blossoms. In the example on the previous page, thick threads were used to make chunky French knots and finer threads to make smaller ones, thus suggesting the variety of textures found in lichen on a rock.

In some cases, you might wish instead to suggest a more clearly defined pattern, perhaps those of the façade of a building, or the markings on a butterfly's wing. Or you might wish to create an abstract pattern, using stitches to make areas of tone or colour. Although they will give a little texture to the surface, the stitches in such cases are used primarily as areas of pattern that give the design its structure.

For the sample shown here, which is based on some Victorian ironwork, I have chosen seeding stitches and eyelets. Seeding lends itself very well to flat patterns, and can be used as densely or as sparsely as you like. Interesting effects can be produced by gradually varying the density, or by mixing two or more colours. The latter technique can give the work a 'pointillist' quality similar to

Left: In this abstract design by Alison Shreeve areas of seeding and detached chain stitches contrast with solidly worked areas of Cretan stitch and detached buttonhole.

that developed by the nineteenth-century French painter Georges Seurat. In the work of Seurat, the Impressionists' method of optical mixing of colours (see page 37) was taken a step further, with the use of very precise dots of colour which, from a distance, blend smoothly yet retain a shimmering quality.

Eyelets have a variety of uses, and are often massed to suggest a field of wildflowers. Here, they are used individually.

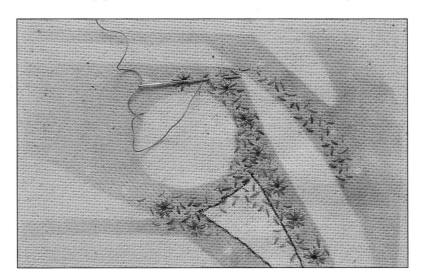

The painted Victorian ironwork of Smithfield Market, in London, provided the subject matter for this piece of stitchery. At an early stage of the work, the transfer-printed shapes are beginning to be filled in with seeding, the rivets depicted with eyelets. Backstitch emphasizes an edge. In the completed work (below) chain stitch gives further definition.

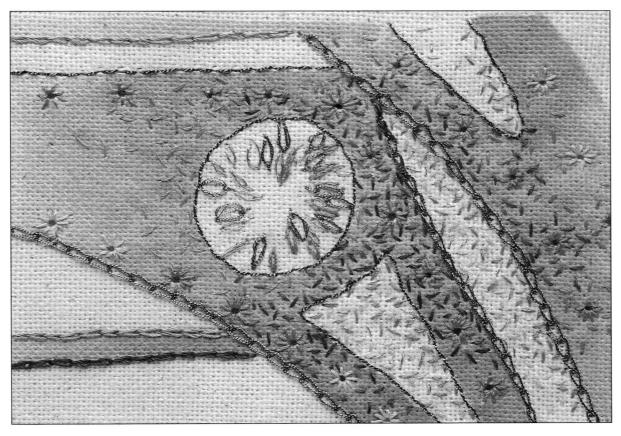

A SMALL GARDEN PICTURE IN STITCHERY

I hope that if you have read thus far and tried some of the stitch experiments your fingers will be itching to begin a real piece of work. You can, of course, choose any subject you like, but I would like to suggest that you begin with a garden scene. Gardens offer plenty of inspiration for the embroiderer in their variety of shapes, colours and textures. You can choose to interpret a garden illustrated in a book, or your own garden or someone else's. The last two options are preferable, for they allow you more scope in selecting a particular area to feature in the work.

It is well worthwhile spending some time looking at various aspects of the garden, either through the lens of a camera or with the help of a sketchbook. You may find that one clump of plants has particular appeal, or that a climbing plant is backed by an interesting wall. You may see

an interesting view by looking through an archway, either natural or constructed. As you look, you need to consider the composition of your picture. It will need to have a foreground, a middle distance and possibly a far distance. It should also have a focal area — an area on which the attention concentrates and where the stitchery will be most densely worked. This area should not be right in the middle of the picture, but preferably just below and to one side of the centre point. By taking a series of photographs, from different vantage points, you will have a choice of compositions, from which you can select the most pleasing.

The next stage is to put on paper, however simply, the image you wish to interpret (see pages 44–48). This will clarify some of the features of your design, because you will concentrate on areas that you like and ignore unnecessary details.

The garden that served as inspiration for the embroidered picture shown here is that of a tiny cottage in Cornwall. From a selection of photographs, I chose one containing a rich variety of colours, with the brightest in the foreground, leading the eye to the statue in the distance, whose grey colour serves as a link with the stones at the lower edge of the picture. I then made a fairly detailed drawing in pastels to serve as a reference for the full-size design.

The two photographs on pages 76 and 77 show the work in two stages: with about one third completed and with all the embroidery worked. When working an embroidery it is important to develop the image gradually over the whole area, rather than finishing one area and moving on to the next. In this way, you can alter various aspects as the work progresses. It is impossible to know in advance what will happen, and you need to be flexible in your approach right up to the last stitch.

Although the stages below refer specifically to this design, you may find some of the methods of working applicable to your own garden picture.

STAGE ONE Using my drawing as a guide, I indicated the main colour areas on another piece of paper using transfer paints. Because the transfer-painted image was rather pale on the beige linen fabric, I added some extra colour using ordinary fabric paint applied with a sponge.

The view of a garden (opposite) served as the inspiration of the project on the following pages. This pastel sketch of the garden was the first stage of the work. It establishes the area and vantage point and highlights the colours and textures to be featured (drawing by Kate Barton).

Bold shapes, such as the rocks in the foreground of this picture, lend themselves to being worked in appliqué (see pages 88–91). For the rocks I chose pieces of grey suede, including two shades to avoid too heavy an effect. These were applied with transfer adhesive.

The statue in the background is also worked in appliqué, but because I did not want it to look too dominant, I chose a lightweight fabric rather than suede. This, too, was bonded to the background.

Having applied these shapes, I next turned to the focal area of the picture, the group of peach-coloured flowers in the lower-right hand quarter of the design. (Notice that I have used artistic licence by substituting peach for the vivid yellow of the marigolds in the photograph; many colour combinations that work well in nature are less successful in art.) I first applied a piece of green-dyed gauze to provide an underlying texture for the foliage, then worked some of the stems in fly stitch, using a variety of thick and thin threads. I carried the fly stitches up and back into the distance, finally adding some scattered fly stitches around the statue to suggest the foliage behind it.

Left: an early stage of the work; here the appliqué shapes have been positioned, some gauze applied to the foreground, and some of the flowers worked.

Opposite: the completed picture. Its feeling of depth has been achieved by working the foreground relatively densely, using the thicker threads and brighter colours.

French knots, loosely worked in fine ribbon, mark the beginning of the development of the focal area.

STAGE TWO   The completed picture has been worked almost entirely in two stitches: French knots and fly stitches. (A few lines of backstitch and several straight stitches have been used to give definition to the statue.) The variety has been achieved by using threads in a great range of colours and textures. The leaves and stems range in colour from pale yellow-green to smoky blue;

the blossoms, from pale cream to soft mauve-pink to peach to intense blue-reds and crimson. Some of the French knots, worked in a single strand of fine embroidery cotton, are the size of pinheads; some of those in the foreground, worked in strips of peach chiffon, are the size of a large pea. Shiny and matt threads are contrasted throughout.

Notice how the stitches blend into each other, and how stitchery has been used to soften the outlines of the stones in the foreground. Notice also that some areas have been left unworked to set off the stitchery and help to suggest depth.

FLAT PATTERN DESIGNS

$\mathcal{A}$nother method of designing is to cut paper shapes and arrange them on the background area, moving them about until you achieve a pleasing design. This method lends itself particularly well to designing for objects of a given shape, such as cushions, quilts, bags and clothing.

The design is planned on a piece of paper marked with the outline of the area to be decorated (or, in the case of a large item such as a quilt, with a scaled-down diagram of it). If the article is clothing, or another three-dimensional object, such as a box, full-size copies of the pattern pieces are used (these should *not* include seam allowance). If the design is to run across a seam, the pieces should be butted together and the motifs positioned so that they match up and flow across the seam. Pieces that overlap — the flap of a bag, for example — should also be positioned as on the finished article so that the design can, if desired, continue from one piece onto the other. Even if the motif will be placed on only one part, the total visible area must be considered in order to ensure that the design is well positioned.

As a general rule, the design should fill most of the background. An exception might be a design going over the shoulder of a jacket, with most of the jacket left plain. Even so, it should echo (however subtly) the part of the shape that it occupies and fill its area comfortably — not float in the space or appear to be stuck on.

Sometimes it may be necessary to distort the original motif slightly in order to make it fit comfortably within the shape. It is also worthwhile to arrange the shapes on some contrasting paper in order to see more clearly the spaces formed between them — the negative shapes. These are an integral part of the design, and can sometimes be more interesting than the motifs themselves. In such a case, you may decide to make these the worked areas of the design, leaving the positive shapes unworked. Or you may simply emphasize them with a few lines of stitching just inside the edges of these areas.

Suitable subjects for flat pattern designing lie all around us. Architecture offers many useful motifs — from simple rectangular forms to fascinating patterns of arches, stone carvings, stairways and rooftops. Ceramic tiles and decorative motifs found on pottery and jewellery are other possibilities. Flowers can also be used. These are most successful if they have interesting silhouettes; but they can often be simplified, distorted, or repeated to make an intriguingly stylized design.

REPEAT DESIGNS   One special kind of flat pattern designing is the repeat pattern, which is described in the following steps. Although the design is a repetition of a single shape, or group of shapes, rather than a free arrangement of different motifs, the basic process is the same as for other kinds of flat pattern designs.

1. Make a tracing of the chosen motif; enlarge it (see page 29) if necessary. Use it as a pattern to cut several identical shapes out of medium-weight paper.

2. Arrange the shapes in several different ways on contrasting paper, noting the spaces formed between them. When you are satisfied with the effect, glue the pieces in place.

3. Make a tracing of the design. It is not always necessary to make a pattern for the complete design, if it will run for some distance; but the repeat should be positioned carefully on the fabric and marked off with pins to make sure it fits. Also, if it turns a corner, the corner must be planned and traced.

4. Transfer the tracing to the fabric by one of the methods described on pages 56–57. If you are working the design in appliqué, use the cut-out shapes as templates for cutting the fabrics.

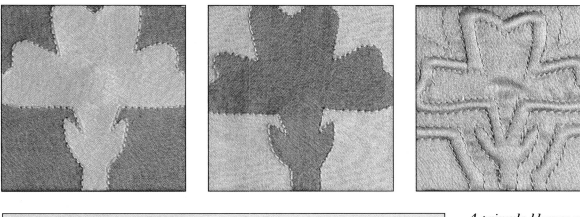

A primula blossom was the point of departure for a project in flat pattern designing by Jean Clarke, several stages of which are shown here.

Opposite: a stylized cutout of the blossom adapted to fit a round shape.

Above: three interpretations of the shape, in shadow quilting (left and centre) and in Italian quilting.

Left: The motif is used as a repeat pattern, trapunto- and Italian-quilted, around the side of a box; individual shadow-quilted motifs line the inner tray.

QUILTING

Quilting is an ancient embroidery technique which is believed to have been developed as a means of keeping warm. Some of the earliest examples (dating to the first century BC) have been found in frozen graves in Siberia. Quilted garments were also worn by knights during the Middle Ages to prevent their armour from chafing. In museums today one can find many examples of quilting from the late seventeenth and early eighteenth centuries. It was fashionable (as well as practical, in those days of minimal heating) for gentlemen to wear elaborate waistcoats which were heavily embroidered and quilted, and for ladies to wear quilted underskirts made of silk. Quilted bed-covers became increasingly decorative at this time. The skills involved in making them were taken by English and other European colonists to America, where they evolved their own techniques and designs, generally used in conjunction with patchwork.

In Britain, during the late eighteenth and nineteenth centuries, quilting flourished especially in Wales and in the area around Durham. The quilters used metal templates in the shape of scrolls, feathers and hearts. These motifs were transferred to the fabric by scratching around the template with a blunt needle — a technique that requires great skill, as the fabric will stay marked for only a short while.

Quilting has many uses in embroidery today. It is still used for functional items such as cushions, jackets, bags and bedcovers, but it also has a purely decorative role, giving fabrics a three-dimensional look which can indicate the textures of carvings and some plants, for example, better than any other embroidery technique. Besides the familiar English quilting, which is padded throughout, Italian and trapunto quilting have become popular; and shadow quilting (see page 108) is used to create very subtle effects.

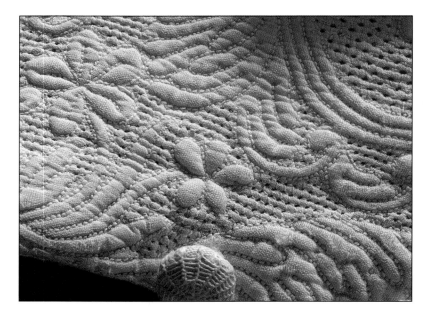

Above: The eight-pointed star-within-a-star that forms the centre of this quilt is typical of the work of Elizabeth Sanderson, who designed and worked it in Northumberland around the turn of the century. The intricate patterns used for the quilting include foliage, flowers and a scrolled border motif.

Opposite: This detail from a quilted waistcoat, made in England early in the eighteenth century, shows the use of backstitch and also the varied relief effects that are produced by altering the density of the quilting.

Designs for quilting are best done by the flat pattern method, and the design transferred either by a tracing or by drawing around templates. The important thing to remember when designing for quilting is that the lines of stitching should be fairly evenly distributed over the fabric, neither very close together nor far apart. This is particularly true of English quilting, in which lines of stitching worked close together will flatten the texture and contrast oddly with the puffier, unstitched areas.

ENGLISH QUILTING

This type of quilting is padded throughout and consists of three layers. The fabric for the top layer needs to be soft and closely woven. Medium-weight, smooth-finished silk, cotton or wool are all suitable. Ideally the fabric should have a slight sheen, which will enhance the texture of the work; satin and shot, or iridescent, fabrics are ideal. On a light-coloured fabric the shadows cast by the quilting show up better than they do on a dark one. Some unconventional materials that also give good results include fine jersey (knits) and soft leather.

The middle layer is the wadding (batting), which is now usually made of polyester. This

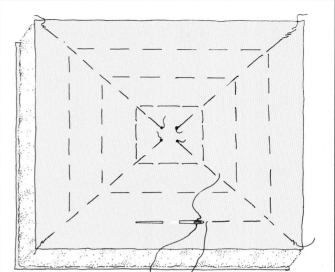

Left: This sample of English quilting, based on a fossil shell, has been worked on iridescent fabric over 4-ounce wadding, using backstitch.

Right: the central motif of Julia Walker's splendid 'Flaneswood Morris' quilt, based on a design by William Morris. The swirling flowers and leaves were applied with silk paints (having first been outlined with a resist). Running stitch was used for the quilting, worked in broken lines to enhance the free, flowing quality of the design.

Above: the layers of fabric and wadding assembled for English quilting being tacked (basted) together.

comes in various thicknesses. In Britain it is available in 2-, 4- and 8-ounce weights, the 4-ounce (about 1.5 cm [⅝ inch] thick) being the most widely used. In the United States, thinner batting is more popular, and the different weights are categorized by such terms as 'low-loft' and 'extra-loft'. The extra-loft is about half as thick as the British 4-ounce, though somewhat denser. A thicker effect can, of course, be achieved by putting two layers together.

The backing fabric should be lightweight, but firm enough to be stretched on a frame and to support the work so that the quilted texture will stand up prominently on the right side. Cotton muslin (not the heavy, unbleached kind) works well for most purposes.

The thread used can be quilters' thread (available from specialist quilting shops), which is a strong, lustrous thread, either all cotton or cotton-wrapped polyester, treated to resist knotting. For a more pronounced line of stitching, use buttonhole twist or a twisted silk or cotton embroidery thread.

A short 'between' needle is the traditional choice for hand quilting, but a slightly longer crewel needle can be used if preferred.

Hand quilting is best worked on a frame, which helps to keep the layers in place. Large quilting frames are suitable for quilts, but smaller projects can be mounted on an ordinary rectangular frame of a convenient size.

For marking the design, a water-erasable pen can be used (first tested on the fabric to make sure it can be removed completely). A silver pencil or a soapstone marker (both available from some specialist shops, especially those in the U.S.) will leave a very faint line which is covered by the stitching.

HAND-QUILTFD CUSHION COVER

The instructions that follow, although specifically intended for a cushion, such as the one shown here, apply generally to other hand-quilted projects.

1 Decide on the size of the finished cushion cover; it should be slightly smaller than the cushion pad (pillow form) so that it will look well filled.

2 Work out the design full size on a piece of paper, using the flat pattern method (see page 78). Choose motifs that have simple shapes, without intricate details, which would flatten the texture.

3 Cut out the three layers of fabric, adding at least 5 cm (2 inches) all around to the size of the finished cover. The wadding (batting) should be a 4-ounce weight (extra-loft or two layers of low loft).

4 Transfer the design onto the top fabric by drawing around paper templates or by the prick and pounce method (see page 56).

5 Attach the backing fabric firmly to a wooden frame, then lay the wadding (batting) and, finally, the top fabric on top of it. Tack (baste) the layers carefully together, starting from the centre and working outwards as shown. The tacking will prevent the fabrics from moving while work progresses.

6 Fasten the thread on the underside, and begin stitching the design, using an appropriate thread. The stitching can be either running or backstitch — which gives a solid line — and needs to be very even in order to look attractive. The stitches should be approximately 3 mm (⅛ inch) long to give the neatest effect. It is best to work with a vertical, stabbing movement, rather than making whole stitches with one movement, which can be difficult with the fabrics in a frame. (However, some quilters, when working on thin wadding, prefer to work running stitches with a sewing movement, keeping the fabric slightly slack in the frame.)

7 When all the quilting has been worked, remove the tacking (basting) stitches and take the work off the frame. Make up the cover as described on page 139.

Right: The sun motif for this quilted cushion was created by the flat pattern method. Segments of three irregular rings, cut from coloured paper, were moved around on the background (on which the sun and radiating lines had first been positioned) until a satisfying arrangement was obtained. The quilting was worked in running stitch, using coton à broder, on raw silk. (Designed by Eleanor Lee, worked by Jean Edwards.)

ITALIAN QUILTING

In this type of quilting the design is formed of double, parallel lines of stitching, worked through two layers of fabric to form a channel, which is then filled with yarn or cord to produce a relief effect. Suitable fabrics for the top and backing are the same as those used for English quilting. A special quilting yarn, made of soft lambswool, is available for this purpose, but you can, instead, use a chunky knitting yarn. Backstitch is used in this work, for a well-defined outline.

1 Mark the design on the top fabric. Where two lines cross, make sure to indicate clearly which line is on top.
2 Tack (baste) the layers together (only a few lines are required), and mount them on a frame.
3 Work the quilting lines in backstitch, using an appropriate thread.
4 Remove the work from the frame. Thread a length of quilting yarn (about 40 cm [16 inches]) onto a bodkin. Working on the wrong side, insert the bodkin and yarn through the backing fabric in one of the

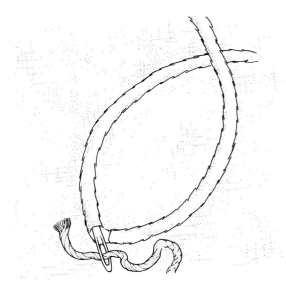

channels. Pull it through the channel. When you reach a corner, bring the bodkin up, then re-insert it in the same hole, following the new direction, leaving a small loop of yarn on the wrong side. Where the channel is crossed by another, bring the yarn up, cut it, leaving a short end, and continue on the other side. The yarn ends can be sewn in place afterward.

Right: Italian and trapunto quilting have been combined in this sample, based (like the English-quilted one on page 82) on a fossil shell.

Above, right: the underside of Italian quilting, showing how channels are overlapped. The stitching is the wrong side of backstitch, which must be used for this linear type of quilting.

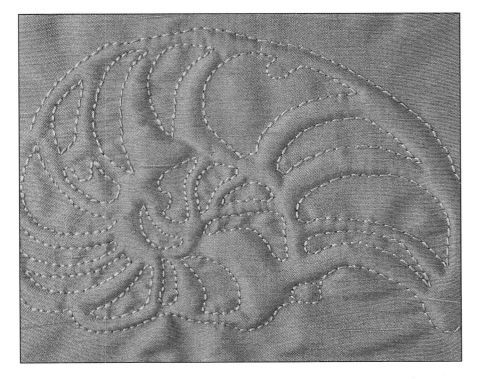

TRAPUNTO QUILTING

Like Italian quilting, trapunto is composed of two layers of fabric, with only certain areas padded; the difference is that in trapunto the padded areas are shapes rather than lines. The two methods are often combined in one piece of work.

Prepare the fabrics and stitch the design as for Italian quilting, steps 1–3. To pad the motifs, first cut a small slit in the backing fabric. Using a bodkin or tapestry needle, insert a small amount of padding, which can be either polyester stuffing or bits of wadding — *not* cotton wool (absorbent cotton). Make sure the shape is padded smoothly, but not tightly. Sew up the slits with herringbone stitch.

QUILTING BY MACHINE

Quilting has traditionally been done by hand; but some delicate, yet hardwearing, results can be achieved on the sewing machine. For large areas of quilting, suitable for a jacket, for example, a method known as random quilting is probably the easiest to use. With the presser foot on the machine, lines are stitched with straight or zigzag stitching. By varying the distances between the lines, some interesting textural effects can be

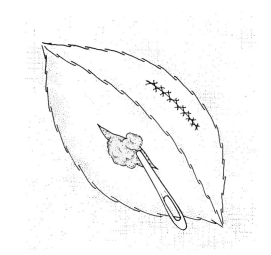

Inserting the stuffing into a trapunto-quilted motif.

produced. For more accurate stitching, it is necessary to remove the foot from the machine and work as described on page 96. This requires some practice, but the effects are well worth the effort.

Machine quilting can be worked on plain fabric, but especially attractive effects can be created if you first colour the fabric with liquid fabric paints, so that the colours run into one another. This will give an interesting background on which to work. The examples shown here were both derived from a picture of rock strata.

Left: This sample of random machine quilting was based on the photograph of rock strata shown opposite, above. The flowing lines were achieved with the presser foot still on the machine.

Opposite: A more faithful interpretation of the rock textures has been created here in free running stitch, without the foot, on a background in which a resist was used to give more definition to the painted areas. A few beads have been added to accentuate the texture.

RANDOM QUILTING

1 Place the top fabric over the wadding (batting) and tack (baste) them together. (A backing fabric is not used, because it tends to cause puckering.)

2 Place the work, unframed, on the machine, with the presser foot attached. Work the stitching, using a normal stitch length for the straight stitching and different width settings for the zigzag lines. For purely decorative work, like the examples shown, you may wish to depart from the usual rule and vary the distances between the lines, so that some areas are much flatter than others.

FREE MACHINE QUILTING For more complex designs, remove the ordinary presser foot and attach the darning foot. Work the design in free running stitch (see page 97).

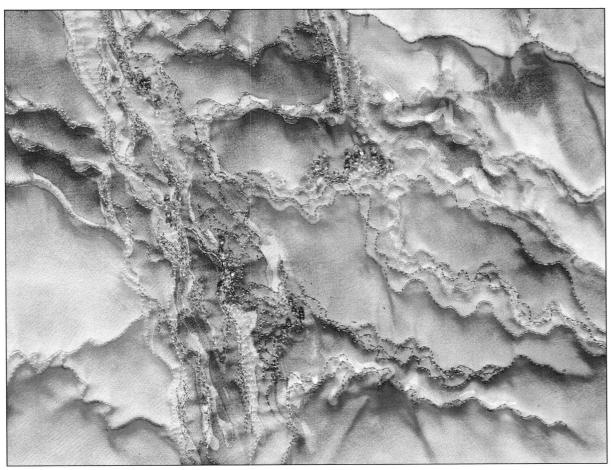

APPLIQUÉ

Another technique that lends itself to the flat pattern method of designing is appliqué. The cut paper shapes will give a fairly realistic impression of the finished effect, especially if they are cut from paper of the same colour or tonal value as the appliqué fabrics. Subtle effects can be achieved by overlaying opaque fabric shapes with sheer ones, which can be suggested in the design stage with tissue paper. When the design has been finalized and traced, for transferring onto the main fabric, the paper shapes can be used as templates for the motifs.

One can easily see why appliqué has been, for centuries, a popular embroidery technique. It is a relatively quick and effective way of placing a contrasting shape or image on a background and can easily be worked large scale if required. These qualities made it especially useful in the Middle Ages for the decoration of knights' surcoats and horse trappings; the colours and symbols made the combatants readily identifiable on a battle-field. For similar reasons, appliqué has traditionally been used to decorate ecclesiastical vestments with religious symbols, intended to be seen from a distance, as in a great cathedral.

In the sixteenth century, when secular embroidery was flourishing as never before, intricate pieces of canvas embroidery (needlepoint) known as 'slips' were applied to rich velvet curtains and bed hangings. Examples of this work can be seen in the Victoria and Albert Museum, in London, and at Hardwick Hall, in Derbyshire.

There are many ways of working appliqué. The method chosen depends on the types of fabric being used, the use of the finished article and the overall effect required. If the object is to be functional, and thus needs to be hard-wearing, flat machine appliqué using zigzag stitch to hold the motifs in place, will be the most suitable. This will be appropriate for items such as cushions, blinds (window shades), bags and children's clothing. For a less hard-wearing item the appliqué can be done by hand, but it will not be quite so strong. If the item is to be washable, the fabrics must all be chosen with this in mind. There are several fabrics which are not washable but are excellent for decorative work. Felt and leather, for example, will not fray and can be applied by hand or machine.

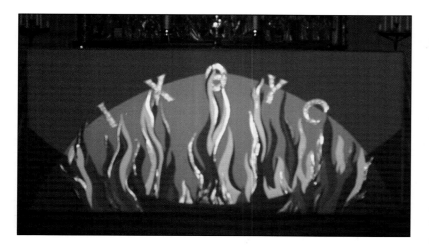

This altar frontal, designed by Jane Lemon, shows the use of appliqué to convey symbolic messages. Here the flames of Pentecost rise up over a fish shape, a symbol derived from the fact that the Greek letters shown, (which stand for 'Jesus Christ, God's Son, Saviour') spell the Greek word for 'fish'.

Opposite: one of the canvaswork slips worked by Mary Queen of Scots and applied to the Oxburgh Hangings.

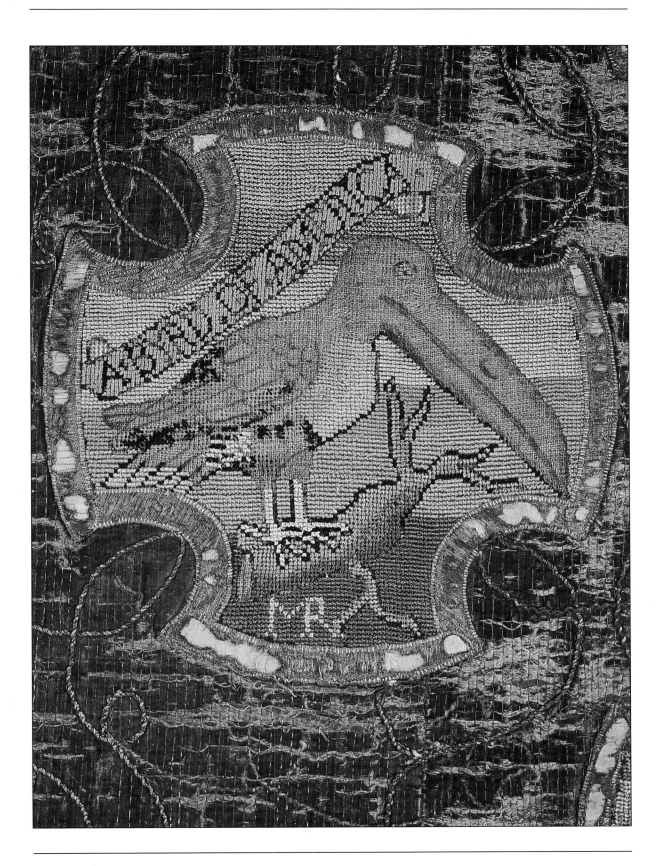

APPLIQUÉ BY HAND

The traditional method of hand appliqué is the turned and stitched method. This should be used on fabrics that fray, unless the work is a decorative panel, in which a slightly frayed edge may be desirable.

1. Place the paper template on the fabric, right side up, and draw around it with tailor's chalk or a soft pencil. It is a good idea to mark the template with an arrow indicating the true vertical of the design, so that the motif can be cut with the straight grain matching that of the background fabric. In some decorative work, however, you may wish to break this rule in order to achieve special effects — for example with iridescent fabrics.
2. Cut out the motif, adding 5 mm (¼ inch) turning allowance. Clip any curved edges to within 2 mm (less than ⅛ inch) of the finished edge.
3. Tack (baste) the motif to the background fabric — not too close to the edges — and sew it in place with tiny slipstitches, turning under the raw edge as you go. (If the fabric is springy, you may prefer to turn under and tack [baste] the edges before applying the motif.)

Using interfacing For larger motifs you may wish to cut the motif first from fusible interfacing, omitting the turnings, then iron this to the wrong side of the fabric and cut out the shape, adding the turnings. This helps to keep the work flat during stitching, but makes the fabric somewhat thicker.

FABRICS THAT DO NOT FRAY may be cut the same size as the template and stab-stitched in place over the edges. A fabric that does fray can be attached by this method if it is first backed with interfacing, and if the item will not be washed.

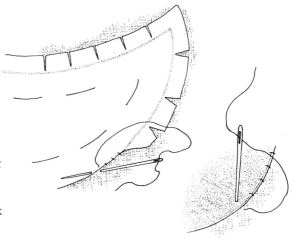

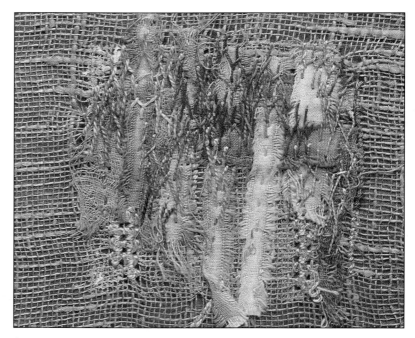

Right: In appliqué of a purely decorative nature, fraying edges are not a problem, and can even be exploited. In this piece by Annwyn Dean, the fabrics are held in place with a variety of stitches, including running and Cretan; the frayed edges contribute to the organic quality of the work.

APPLIQUÉ BY MACHINE

This is much more hard-wearing than hand appliqué. For best results, match the grain of the motif to the grain of the background fabric. In the case of large-scale work, such as banners, the motif should be lockstitched to the background before the edges are stitched, in order to hold it smoothly in place. (Consult a book on household furnishings for instructions for working lockstitch.) Surface stitchery worked over the applied motif will have the same effect.

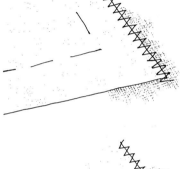

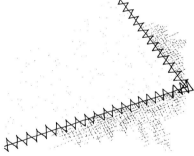

The stitch I prefer to use for machine appliqué is a slightly open zigzag; this is more attractive than satin stitch, I feel, as it is not so heavy (although satin stitch can be effective if the width is varied, as in the example shown below); and it is just as hard-wearing. Make a sample first to determine the best width and length of stitch for your fabric.

1. Mark and cut out the fabric shape, using the template, omitting the turning allowance.
2. Tack (baste) the shape to the background fabric; or, if it is very small, pin it in place.
3. Set the machine for zigzag stitch of an appropriate size, and position the motif on the machine with the edge centred under the foot. Begin stitching, making sure that the needle pierces each fabric in turn. At corners, pivot the fabric with the needle in it, on an 'outside' swing, so that the zigzag stitching will be reinforced at that point.

Right: Machine appliqué need not have a mechanical appearance, as this graceful floral embroidery by Beryl Court proves. The flowers and leaves are applied and defined with close zigzag and satin stitch. Lines of free running stitch (see page 97) help to soften and integrate the edges.

FREE APPLIQUÉ

For purely decorative work, it is possible to apply fabrics by means of a material known as transfer adhesive, or transfer fusing web. This bonds the motif to the background fabric, eliminating the need for stitching — although in most cases some surface stitchery to enhance the work will be desirable.

1. Trace the motif, reversed, onto the paper side of the adhesive, and cut it out.
2. Place the transfer adhesive motif on the wrong side of the fabric and press it in place, using a hot, dry iron and a damp cloth.
3. Cut around the shape and then peel away the paper.
4. Position the motif on the background fabric, and press it in place, using a damp cloth as before.

For this method, you need not transfer the outlines of the design onto the background fabric. Simply move the fabric shapes around on the background, following your cut-paper design — or departing from it if you like — and fix them to it, overlapping them where appropriate. Because the adhesive prevents fraying, some of the motifs can be attached lightly, with the point of the iron, and then caught more securely with a few decorative stitches.

THREE-DIMENSIONAL APPLIQUÉ

Nothing could be more unlike the crisp, clearly defined shapes of traditional appliqué than three-dimensional appliqué. In this innovative version of the technique, fabrics are gathered, scrunched up and overlaid to create fascinating textures that suggest vegetation and other natural forms.

The fabrics used for this type of work should include some that are transparent or loosely woven, so that the underlying layers will be partly visible. The finished effect should be one of unity, in which the different fabrics seem to grow out of one another.

EDGES   There are various ways of treating the edges of the fabrics used for three-dimensional appliqué so that they will blend into the work.

Fraying   Deliberately fray the raw edges of the fabric shapes to give a soft outline. This is most easily done on fairly loosely woven fabrics.

Adhesive   Paint a line of PVA glue, or the resist used with liquid fabric paints, in a wavy line along the edge to be cut. When the adhesive has dried, cut along the line of adhesive to seal the edge of the fabric.

Burning   This technique should be used with care, especially on synthetic fabrics, but is quite safe if carried out near a bowl of water. Light a candle (first place in a candle holder), and run the edges of the fabric along the flame so that it just scorches. If the fabric chars, this can be crumbled away after it has cooled.

Machine-made lace   This will give a lacy edge to appliqué fabrics and can look very effective, so long as some of the stitching is worked onto the fabric and not just off the raw edges. The technique for working machine lace is given on pages 112–115.

After the edges are treated, the fabrics are applied by hand or machine, ruched and overlapped in a way that will conceal any untreated edges. On some designs the treated edges may be left hanging free.

Opposite: Some bright pink geraniums (left) provided the subject matter for a little piece of free appliqué (right).

Opposite, above: applying a motif, backed with transfer adhesive, to the background fabric.

Left: This example of three-dimensional appliqué by Rosemary Dobson was inspired by peeling paint on an old door.

MACHINE EMBROIDERY

Machine embroidery is one of the most popular forms of embroidery today – for several reasons. Once you have mastered the basic skills, which are few, you will find this technique not only quick but extremely versatile. With it, you can produce delicate stitchery, finer than you could achieve by hand, yet, at the same time, quite hard-wearing.

Many people are unsure what machine embroidery is, and erroneously think it beyond the capability of their own domestic sewing machine. The manufacturers would like you to believe that you need a sophisticated computerized model with dozens of electronic stitch patterns, from rose borders to repeating ducks. These stitch patterns are indeed very useful for decorating items such as table napkins or the hems of skirts, but they have limited uses, as they will produce embroidery only in straight lines and uniform shapes.

Free machine embroidery — the subject of this chapter — is totally different and much more crea-

tive. You do not need a special machine for it. The only requirements are that the machine must be electrically operated (leaving both hands free to move the fabric) and that it have a swing needle, in order to make a zigzag stitch. Even this is not essential, but it greatly increases the possibility of making different stitch textures.

If you are planning to buy a new machine, I suggest that you buy the least expensive model offered by a top manufacturer. This will usually provide the basic functions for dressmaking and household furnishings, but will also have sufficient adaptability to cope with the different types of fabric that we use in machine embroidery today. Some machines do not like stitching without the presser foot (the usual method in free machine embroidery), and in this case, it is worthwhile trying the darning foot, which will hold the fabric in place when the needle goes into it. In any case, it is a good idea to do some practice exercises on your present machine before rushing out to buy a new one.

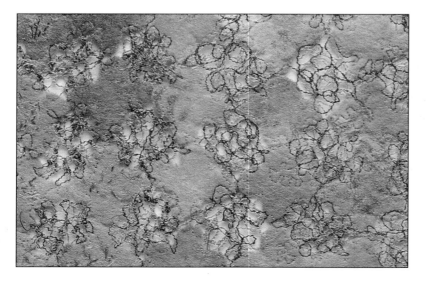

Left: The spontaneity of machine embroidery is illustrated by this detail from a wall hanging by Linda Chilton, based on Islamic motifs, which has been worked on painted felt and dissolving fabric in free running stitch.

Right: materials and equipment needed for machine embroidery. Note that the presser foot of the machine has been removed and the feed dog covered with a special plate. The darning foot (foreground) can be used, if required. The threads shown are just a few of those that can be used for this work. A spring-type ring frame is most convenient; here it holds fabric that has been painted to provide a guide for stitching.

MATERIALS AND EQUIPMENT

FRAMES A frame is usually essential for free machine embroidery, as the fabric must be kept taut in order for the top thread to pick up the bobbin thread to form the stitch. A ring frame (see photograph) is used for machine embroidery. It must be shallow enough – 1 cm (⅜ inch) or less – to slip under the needle, and not too large; I recommend one 15 cm (6 inches) in diameter. The metal and plastic spring frame produced by Elna is useful, as it has small teeth which grip the fabric firmly. The advantage of a spring-type frame is that it can be moved from one area to another while the work is in progress. Otherwise, you can use a narrow wooden frame, first binding the inner ring with woven tape, so as to hold the fabric firmly.

FABRICS Many different fabrics can be used for machine embroidery; but if you are a beginner it is important to choose a fabric that is easy to stitch on, so as to avoid any unnecessary problems while you are still mastering the basic techniques. Choose a fabric with a plain weave – one that is neither so loosely woven that it may snag nor so tightly woven that the needle may bounce off it. Calico (unbleached muslin) is ideal for practice. Other medium-weight cottons and fabrics made of other natural fibres are also good. Synthetics may repel the needle, and stretchy fabrics, such as jerseys (knits), are also difficult to work on.

THREADS Although you can use ordinary sewing threads for machine work, it is best to use the special machine embroidery threads available. These are finer and more lustrous than ordinary sewing threads. The higher the number, the finer the thread. They are usually made of cotton or rayon and are lovely to use, as they easily run through the needle at speed. Thick threads, such as those used for hand embroidery, can be used in the bobbin or couched onto the fabric.

NEEDLES You do not need special needles for machine embroidery; but as with ordinary sewing, it is important to use the correct size needle for the thread that you are using. For most machine embroidery threads, size 80 (11) or 90 (14) is suitable. For some of the thicker metallic threads it will be necessary to use a larger needle, such as size 100 (16).

STARTING MACHINE EMBROIDERY

You will find that it takes a few hours of practice to get the feel of free machine embroidery. For your first exercises, you can, if you wish, just make squiggles on some plain fabric. But you may find it helpful — and more enjoyable — to work on fabric to which you have first applied some fabric paint. The areas of colour will provide an interesting background for the stitching and give the work a measure of coherence, even at this early stage. Take a large piece of calico (unbleached muslin), and apply the paints in an abstract design, using sweeping strokes (see page 51). (After you have mastered the basic skill of guiding the frame, you could first apply a gutta resist to the fabric, and then the paint; this would provide a pattern of lines to use as a guide when stitching.) You can then either cut the fabric into 20-cm (8-inch) squares to practise on individually or leave it whole and re-mount it in the frame as required when one area has been filled with stitching.

Before you start stitching, it will be necessary to make a few adjustments to the sewing machine:

1. Remove the presser foot. Attach the darning foot if required. (Sometimes, for a large piece of work, or if several layers of fabric are being used, it will be impractical to use the embroidery frame; and in this case, the darning foot will help to hold the fabric flat.)
2. Lower the feed dog teeth by setting the machine for 'darning', following the machine instruction book. On some machines a special plate is provided for covering the teeth.
3. Set the stitch width dial to '0' (for free running stitch; see below). The stitch length can be set at any point, since the actual length will be controlled by you.
4. Insert a suitable needle, and thread up the machine in the normal way.
5. Mount the fabric in a ring frame, making sure that it is as taut as possible.
6. Place the fabric under the needle, and lower the presser bar in order to engage the top thread tension. (When the foot is off, this step is easily overlooked; if you have problems, check that the lever is down.)
7. Bring the bobbin thread to the surface of the fabric by holding onto the top thread and turning the fly wheel (on the right of the machine) towards you.
8. Making sure that you are in a comfortable position and not crouched over the machine, hold both threads in one hand and make a few stitches on the spot to fasten the thread. Cut off the loose ends.

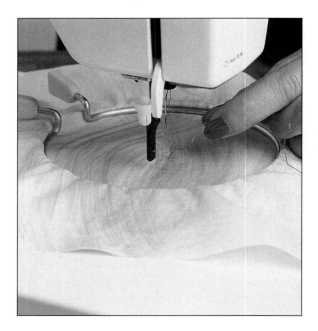

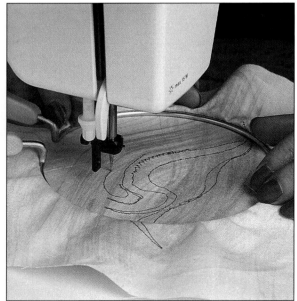

9. Hold the frame as shown, with your fingers well out of the way. Run the machine fast and, at the same time, move the frame very slowly from front to back, from side to side, and in circles. It will seem strange at first having so little control over your work, but you will soon find that you can make circles at will without any jerky movements.

If by chance the thread or — worse — the needle breaks, it is because the frame has been moved too quickly. Just replace the thread or needle, take a few deep breaths, relax your shoulders, and try again.

FREE RUNNING STITCH This is essentially machine straight stitch, but worked freely as described above. It is the basic stitch of machine embroidery and has the flattest of textures. On some fabrics, such as felt, the stitches will sink into the fabric, giving an almost quilted effect. It can be used with wadding (batting) underneath to do free machine quilting (see page 87). This has a much more delicate quality than hand quilting because the stitches are so small. Free running stitch is used where lines are needed, so it is most effective when used to interpret drawings with a flat quality. Closely spaced lines can be used inside and outside the edge of an appliqué shape that has been applied with transfer adhesive (fusing web) to finish the raw edges and integrate the shape into the background fabric.

ZIGZAG STITCH By adjusting the stitch width lever, you can make the needle move automatically from side to side in a zigzag pattern of a fixed width, while you control the stitch length. If you move the frame quickly, an open zigzag will result; if you move it slowly, a satin stitch will be formed. You might make a small sampler of lines worked in free running and zigzag stitch. By moving the position of the width lever and altering the speed of the frame, you can produce a variety of different types of line.

Left: These lines of free running and zigzag stitch have been worked on a smooth fabric.

Below: When worked on felt, the stitches sink into the fabric, producing an effect similar to quilting.

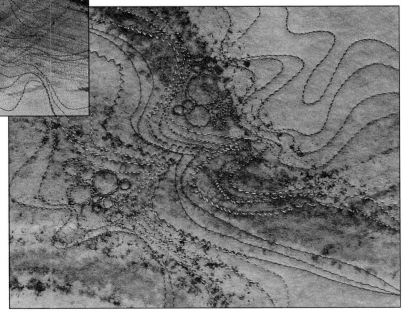

Opposite, left: pulling the bobbin thread up to the surface.

Opposite, right: working the stitching. Lines of free running stitch are shown, along with some open zigzag.

TEXTURES IN MACHINE EMBROIDERY

Having tried the basic stitches of machine embroidery, you will have discovered just how much practice is needed in order to make marks where you want them and not where the machine dictates. Try not to be frightened of the machine. Remember that it is only a tool; with practice you will be able to make it do what *you* want!

Besides making lines of stitching, your sewing machine is also capable of producing some exciting textures to enrich the surface of the fabric. This can be done either by changing the tension settings of the machine or by using some thicker threads, such as those normally used for hand stitchery. It is well worthwhile experimenting with all of these techniques, for you will find some more successful than others on your machine. You may also find that it takes a while to achieve results with techniques that involve altering the tension settings. It is all a question of understanding how your machine works and gaining confidence in its use.

WHIP STITCH   This gives a slightly raised texture to the stitchery and is achieved by pulling the bobbin thread through to the surface while stitching. This thread appears to wrap itself around the top thread, giving a slightly corded effect. Whip stitch can be achieved by several methods. In practice, all of them may be necessary.

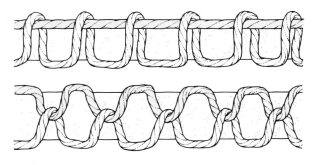

Above: a cross-section drawing of normal machine stitching.
Top: the bobbin tension loosened for whip stitch.

- Reduce the bobbin tension by slightly loosening the screw on the bobbin case which holds the tension spring in position. Take care that the screw does not come out completely, as it is very easily lost. It is best to purchase a spare bobbin case to keep for embroidery, so that the other one remains intact for everyday use.

- Use a stronger thread in the needle and a weaker one in the bobbin. This will help to pull the bobbin thread through without altering the tension. A suitable combination would be machine embroidery cotton No. 30 on the top with machine embroidery cotton No. 50 or rayon No. 30 in the bobbin.

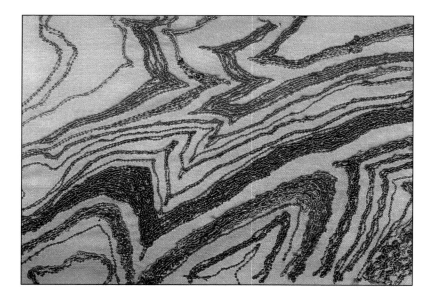

Left: a sample of whip stitch based on the contours of a map. The looped texture is produced by a relatively slack lower tension, which brings the bobbin thread up to whip the top thread.

Opposite: this detail of a machine-embroidered panel, based on studies of an azalea plant, incorporates a variety of textures, including whip stitch and cable stitch, as well as applied pieces of fabric.

- Increase the top tension. Your machine instruction book will probably mention a 'universal tension' and show the correct setting for this. You should keep the dial at this setting for normal stitching; but if you set it to a higher number or towards the 'plus' sign, the top thread will tend to pull the lower thread through to the surface.

CABLE STITCH   This gives quite a chunky texture. A hand embroidery thread, such as perlé cotton, soft (matte) embroidery cotton or a metallic crochet yarn, is used in the bobbin. The top thread is usually a machine embroidery cotton or rayon, and the work is done on the reverse of the fabric.

1. Wind the thick thread onto the bobbin, using the bobbin winder on the machine to make sure it is wound evenly. Only short lengths can be used at a time, because the bobbin will jam if it is too full.

2. The lower tension must be bypassed. Depending on the machine, this is done either by threading the bobbin thread through a hole at the back of the bobbin case or by unscrewing the tension spring to a loose position before inserting the bobbin.

3. Place the fabric in a frame with the wrong side uppermost. Position it on the machine, and pull the thick thread through to the surface. If this proves difficult, a stiletto can be used to make a hole in the fabric. Holding onto both threads, begin stitching. You can use either free running stitch or zigzag, which will produce wide lines of textural stitchery.

COUCHING   It is possible to use virtually any thread for machine embroidery. If it is too thick to be wound onto the bobbin, it can be couched onto the surface of the fabric. The method is similar to couching by hand (see page 67) but much quicker to do, and the result is stronger and more hard-wearing.

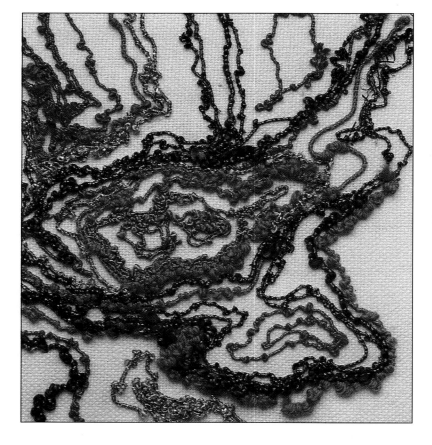

Left: a sample of cable stitch. These thicker threads were used in the bobbin and the embroidery worked from the wrong side.

Opposite, above: working a sample of couching. The needle is taken across the couched thread at intervals. A toothpick is used to guide the thread, protecting the fingers.

Opposite, below: The completed sample shows the variety of threads that can be used in this technique.

100

1. Thread up the machine with the same machine embroidery thread top and bottom, preferably in a colour matching the thread to be couched. Return both tensions to normal, and check that the machine is stitching evenly.
2. Position the thread to be couched on the fabric; make a few stitches in place to anchor it.
3. Holding the frame with one hand and guiding the thread with a cocktail stick, as shown, to keep your fingers away from the needle, stitch alongside the thread, then move the frame slightly to one side to take the needle over the thread. Continue stitching along the other side for a short distance, then make another couching stitch back to the first side. Continue in this way. Trim the loose ends of the couched threads.

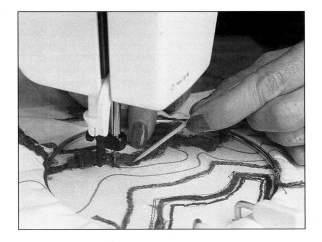

The couched thread should not be flattened by the stitching, but should retain its original characteristics, with the stitches holding it invisibly in place. The thread can also be looped in order to give exaggerated textures, and a variety of different threads and strips of fabric can be combined to create different effects.

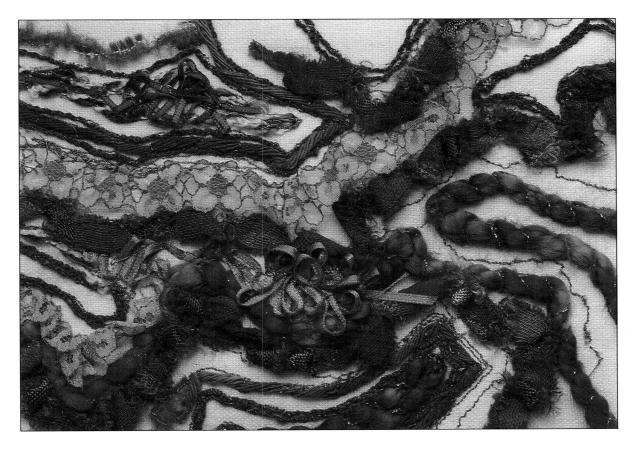

CONTRASTING
MACHINE-EMBROIDERED TEXTURES

It is rare that one would work any one machine embroidery technique in isolation. The illustrations on these pages show a variety of techniques, used to provide sufficient contrast between the textured and flat areas. Before embarking on a piece of work, it is always a good idea to make some samples using a combination of different techniques to see which will be the most suitable. Some exciting discoveries can often be made at this stage; conversely, the unsuitability of a technique for the fabric and/or thread will quickly become evident.

INCORPORATING APPLIQUÉ AND
HAND STITCHING

Machine embroidery looks best when used in conjunction with other techniques. It is helpful to use a fabric on which the design is first painted; this will act as a guide in placing the stitching. It is also often helpful to have some areas of applied fabrics, especially where a large part of the background has been painted one colour. This will give a welcome variation in texture; and the machine stitching, in turn, will help to blend the appliqué shapes into the background and will soften any hard edges.

Materials used for appliqué can include almost

Left: The complementary potential of machine and hand stitching are shown in this detail from an embroidered panel. The machine is capable of producing wonderfully intricate and spontaneous patterns, which here provide a foundation for more emphatic hand stitches.

Opposite: This panel, inspired by a garden in the Cotswolds, shows the use of appliqué, as well as hand stitchery, in a piece of machine embroidery.

anything, from scraps of leather to filmy bits of chiffon cut from old scarves; medical gauze, used for bandages, is often useful, as it can easily be manipulated into different shapes. These fabrics can be built up in layers as required and held in position with transfer adhesive (fusing web). Some of the more transparent fabrics will allow the lower layers to show through, and loosely woven fabrics, such as scrim and gauze, can be pulled to form holes before being applied. Once the layers are bonded together, however loosely, they create a new fabric which can serve as the base for your stitchery. (In most cases this will entail the use of the darning foot, since the fabric texture would be spoiled by being placed in a frame.)

The machine embroidery should be used to enrich this surface, but should not look as if it has been done in a random manner. Scribbles are fine for practice pieces but stand out awkwardly on a finished piece of embroidery. It is important that any stitch you choose should blend in with the background.

Machine embroidery worked in free running stitch or zigzag has a delicate quality and will often require the addition of some heavier stitching to act as a contrast and to create areas of focus. This can be achieved with one or more of the machine techniques described on pages 100–101; but it can also be done effectively with hand stitching. The stitchery is best kept as simple as possible, limited to one or two different stitches, such as straight stitch and French knots. Beads may also be used to embellish further the surface of the embroidery; these are best confined to one or two areas, rather than scattered over the work like confetti.

Left: Machine embroidered flower shapes (some worked on dissolving fabric) have been applied to the centre of this panel. The painted background fabric has been partially cut away and applied to a silver fabric. Machine-couched yarn forms the vines: the flower stems are wrapped cords (see page 122).

A MACHINE-EMBROIDERED PANEL

There is a wealth of texture, pattern and colour to be found in buildings. Closely studied, these form a fascinating source of design inspiration for the embroiderer. It is probably a mistake, however, to try to work from a whole building, because the problems of perspective can be quite daunting (although distant groups of buildings, as in a skyline, are relatively manageable). A more productive approach is to look at some of the details.

First of all, find some interesting buildings, and look at the doors, windows, chimneys and decorative details, such as wrought-iron work. Then look closer still at the texture of the brickwork or stonework. On an old building, this may have become crumbly over the years; it may also have acquired other textures, with outcrops of moss or

Right: Details of buildings, especially those weathered with age, lend themselves well to interpretation in embroidery. This lichen- and ivy-covered house, with its unusual lattice window, would make an excellent subject.

lichen. Look at peeling paintwork, and notice how the colours have become changed by the effect of years of frequent rainfall or hot sunshine. Look at paths and paving, at the interesting patterns that the stones make and at the small plants that may be found nestling between the cracks. It is well worthwhile having a really good look at several different types of building before selecting an area to interpret in embroidery. Your own photographs or drawings of the subject (see pages 27 and 48) will yield material that can serve as the basis of the design. Once you have chosen the area to be used, you may need to enlarge it, as described on page 29.

The machine-embroidered panel shown here is based on an old wooden door set in the wall of a large country garden. The colours and textures of the stonework contrast with the grey wood and the climbing plants.

The embroidery has been photographed at two stages: about half-way through the work and with all the work completed. The accompanying descriptions of the work process may, I hope, give you some ideas that you can adapt when creating your own machine-embroidered panel or wall hanging.

STAGE ONE   For the background of the panel I chose a furnishing fabric, which I painted with fabric paint to give the colours and texture of the stonework. At the same time, I also painted a piece of medical gauze to be used for appliqué shapes.

The wooden door was cut from a piece of grey wool fabric and fixed to the background with transfer adhesive (fusing web) (see page 92). Shapes resembling the stones of the wall were cut from the painted gauze and also applied to the background.

Soft (matte) embroidery cotton was wound onto the bobbin of the machine and cable stitch worked, from the reverse of the fabric, to indicate the texture of lichen on the wall. Cable stitch was also worked with a perlé cotton thread to give a shiny texture in places.

Leaf shapes were cut from pieces of painted silk and organza and backed with transfer adhesive (fusing web), so that they could be attached where needed.

The machine was threaded with dark grey

thread top and bottom, and free running stitch was worked over the door area to suggest the grain lines in the wood.

STAGE TWO   Further cable stitch was added where needed. The machine was threaded up with grey thread, and free running stitch was worked over the wall area to indicate the divisions between the stones.

Some thick knitting yarn was couched by machine to represent the vertical and horizontal lines of the door; then cable stitch and free running stitch were worked in between the lines of couching to soften the effect.

A green loopy yarn was couched along the lower edge of the door to form a base for the plant material; this was softened by the addition of a piece of medical gauze painted green.

The separate leaf shapes previously cut and backed with transfer adhesive (fusing web) were applied with just a touch of the iron so that they remain standing away from the work in places.

Finally, some hand stitchery was added. A few French knots were worked on the stonework; these blend in well with the cable stitch. Fly stitches were worked in soft (matte) embroidery cotton and perlé to suggest some darker green strap-like leaves at the base of the wall.

Opposite: The door has been applied on this panel, some of the wall worked, and some leaves attached.

Above: the completed embroidery. Note the addition of hand stitches, including fly stitch and couching.

MACHINE WORK ON TRANSPARENT FABRICS

So far, we have dealt only with machine embroidery worked on opaque background fabrics, although we have also explored the use of transparent fabrics applied in layers to the background. On many occasions, however, one would want the background itself to be transparent. Sheer fabrics have been used for centuries for various kinds of hand embroidery. Here, I shall be considering some of these techniques as adapted for machine embroidery on these fabrics.

For practical applications, such as embroidery worked on an evening blouse or a wedding veil, careful consideration must be given to the effect of the embroidery on the fabric and the style of the garment or accessory. For example, the stitching on a wedding veil must be light and delicate, so as not to spoil the filmy quality of the fabric. If the item is to be washable — a curtain, for instance, or a blouse – the embroidery, too, must be capable of withstanding frequent launderings.

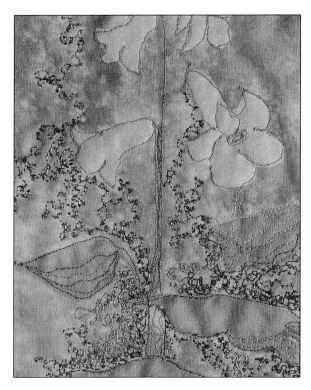

Transparent fabrics can also be effectively used in purely decorative embroidery. In particular, they can be used to suggest certain effects of light, such as fog, haze, or the reflections and distortions we see when looking at an object through glass. The best way of lightly blurring an image in embroidery is through the use of transparent fabrics.

SHADOW QUILTING   In the traditional technique of shadow quilting, small motifs are cut from an opaque fabric and trapped between two layers of transparent fabric, such as organdie. Felt is often used for the motifs, because it gives a slightly raised texture, with little weight, and is non-fraying. However, other fabrics are also suitable — even sheer ones, for an extra-delicate effect. The motifs are held in place with stitching worked through the two outer layers. In hand quilting, backstitch is normally used; in machine quilting, free running (i.e. straight) stitch is the usual choice. If the article being made is to be washable, make sure that all the fabrics used can be laundered in the same way and that they have been pre-shrunk.

For a purely decorative effect, try experimenting with different types of fabric. The technique could be adapted for a panel, using an opaque cotton, for example, for the background, and one or more layers of transparent fabric on top. When the background is opaque, however, the motifs can easily get 'lost' unless they are accentuated in some way. The use of transfer paints can prevent this and will impart additional depth and subtlety to the work.

To get an idea of the effect, paint a random pattern onto a sheet of paper, using a sponge. Iron the design onto the background fabric in the usual way (see page 55). Then make a second printing, from the same paper, onto a piece of polyester voile. Cut some circles from different coloured organza (or another fabric of your choice); place these on the background, and lay the sheer fabric on top. The circles can be held in place with fine pins or a little fabric glue. Set the machine for free running stitch, without the presser foot, and stitch around and among the circles so that they are firmly fixed in place. Surface stitchery can be added by hand, if desired, to give an extra dimension to the work.

Having worked this simple exercise in shadow quilting, you might like to use the technique for a more carefully planned piece of embroidery. Shadow quilting is especially well suited to any subject in which a slightly blurred effect is required. In the embroidery opposite, for example, the flowers are softened by a layer of organza.

Opposite, above: The flower-heads and leaves in this embroidery have been worked in shadow quilting. The painted background shows softly through the voile which forms the top layer of the work.

Opposite, below: This detail from a panel shows embroidered net flowers applied to a background of multi-coloured strips of fabric.

Right: A diamond-paned window was the inspiration for this piece of shadow quilting, which incorporates felt shapes and lengths of ribbon.

NET EMBROIDERY   Embroidery on net became very popular during the nineteenth century, when machines were developed to make the net fabrics; before this time, nets had been made by hand. The embroidery was done in such a way as to simulate lace, and in various parts of Europe different styles developed. Sometimes intricate filling patterns were worked onto the net in a technique known as needlerun net; in others, such as Carrickmacross lace, a type of appliqué was worked, using fine muslin on the net ground. These techniques were worked on hexagonal net or tulle. Another type of net, with a square grid, also began to be mass produced; and it, too, became popular for embroidery. The technique used is known as lacis, or filet darning (netting). It consists of working various stitches over the grid, thus filling in some of the holes to form a pattern or image.

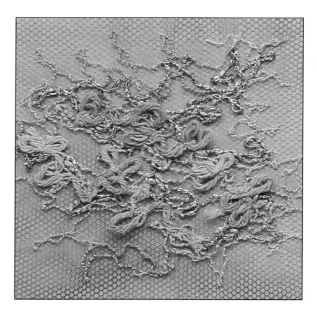

It is a good idea to experiment with different types of net in order to explore the qualities of the different fabrics. A curtain fabric shop, or the curtain fabric department of a good-sized store, will usually have different grades of sheer mesh fabrics, usually made of synthetic fibres. These will take fabric transfer paints well, and interesting effects can be obtained by placing a square mesh over a finer net and ironing through both layers. In the sample shown opposite, I have used several different types of curtain net, cut into rectangles and applied to a fine hexagonal net.

Right: Several sheer and translucent fabrics, applied to a net background, have been enhanced with lines of machine stitching. A few beads provide accents.

Opposite: Cable stitch was worked on this piece of net, then thick dyed threads were machine-couched to add texture. Free running stitch was used to link the areas.

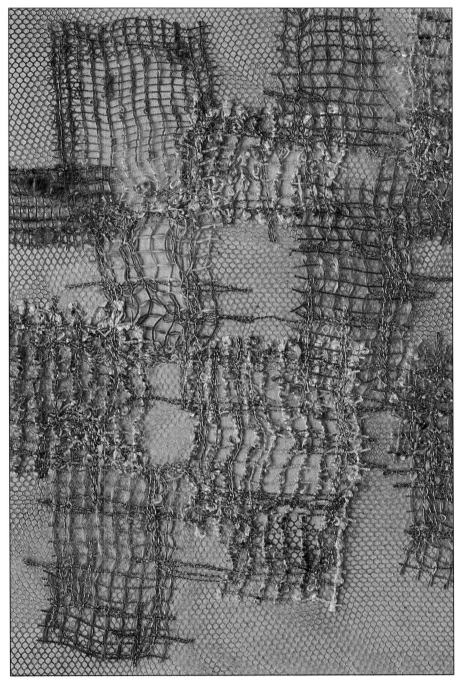

Right: The possibilities of net over net are explored in this embroidery, in which several square curtain nets have been applied to a hexagonal net background. The applied pieces were then decorated with more lines of vertical and horizontal free-running stitch, using a variety of metallic and glossy threads.

Some lovely textures can be obtained by working cable stitch and couching on a net background. However, the nature of the finished embroidery needs to be carefully considered, for too much weight in certain areas will cause the fabric to hang unevenly. It is also important to make sure that densely worked areas are complemented by some flatter unworked areas.

Because net does not fray, it is easy to finish the raw edges; simply work free running stitch along the edge (or zigzag, if you prefer), then trim close to the stitching.

MACHINE-MADE LACE

We have seen how lace can be simulated on the sewing machine by using net as a foundation; but there are some exciting possibilities of creating machine lace fabrics without any visible evidence of a background fabric. These techniques involve working on a water-soluble material. After the stitching is completed, the fabric is dissolved, leaving a delicate piece of machine-made lace.

These water-soluble fabrics are comparatively new; until recently, vanishing muslin was often used as a means of supporting the embroidery. This consists of a chemical gauze, which crumbles away on application of a hot iron. It is not very convenient to use and is not suitable for all types of thread, particularly synthetic and metallic. Another type of fabric used widely in the past is acetate, which is dissolved by being placed in acetone. This works well, as the fabric is easy to stitch onto, but great care is needed when handling the acetone, for it is highly inflammable, and the fumes are dangerous to inhale.

By contrast, the new water-soluble fabrics are easy to use. There are two types: one dissolves in hot water, the other in cold.

Below and below right: tracing a leaf shape onto cold-water soluble fabric and working over the traced lines with free running stitch.

Opposite: Lacy blooms of cow parsley, worked on dissolving fabric and incorporating some sheer fabric, have been applied to a background of rich greenery.

HOT-WATER-SOLUBLE   This is a firmly woven fabric which stays taut in the embroidery ring. After the chosen design has been worked, the fabric is placed in boiling water for a few minutes to dissolve the fibres. The embroidery tends to shrink rather alarmingly but can be pinned out to shape and left to dry after being removed from the hot water with tongs.

COLD-WATER-SOLUBLE   This fabric has a plastic appearance and is completely transparent. It tends to be rather stretchy to sew onto, so may need to be used double. It sometimes tends to tear while being stitched; the use of a ball-point or small (size 70 [9]) needle and the darning foot will help to prevent this. Such precautions are well worth taking, for the fabric is the easiest of all to dissolve. A good method is to pin the completed work to a polystyrene ceiling tile and then dip the whole thing into a bowl of cold water. The fabric disappears completely in a few minutes, and the motif(s) can be left to dry.

WORKING ON COLD-WATER-SOLUBLE FABRIC
1. Trace the chosen design onto the fabric, using a soft pencil.
2. Frame up the fabric and prepare the machine for free running stitch (see pages 96–97).
3. Work the stitching, going over the lines several times, so that they overlap each other, and taking care that all the lines are linked. Any stitching that is not linked will fall apart when the fabric is dissolved.

Machine-made lace can be used in various ways. For example, small pieces can be treated as appliqué shapes and used to enhance the texture of an embroidered panel. Or you can combine several pieces to make three-dimensional objects, such as the flowers shown on page 131.

INCORPORATING OTHER FABRICS   It is quite feasible to apply scraps or even large pieces of material to the dissolving fabric, thus combining the lace with areas of woven fabric. This has many possibilities for experimental work; several layers of fabric and lace can be built up to produce fascinating see-through effects.

4. Cut away the excess fabric from the edges of the design, and pin the work onto a polystyrene tile. Immerse the tile in cold water for several minutes; then remove it from the water and leave it to dry.

1. For your first experiment, choose a shape that is not too complex, such as a skeletonized leaf. Make a simple drawing of the main lines, and trace these onto the soluble fabric. Place a piece of silk under the soluble fabric; tack (baste) it in place.

Above: removing a lace motif (pinned to a polystyrene tile) from a bath of cold water.

Left: several completed motifs. Note that each line has been worked over more than once to provide the necessary body and visibility.

2. Work the main lines in free running stitch. Remove the fabrics from the frame, and cut away the silk in certain places, leaving only the soluble fabric.

3. Work more stitching to indicate the finer veining of the leaf. Pin out the fabric and immerse it, as described above. When the soluble material has dissolved away, you will have a new piece of fabric consisting of scraps of silk held together with a network of lacy stitching.

This technique can be developed by overlaying different types of fabric in the same piece of work.

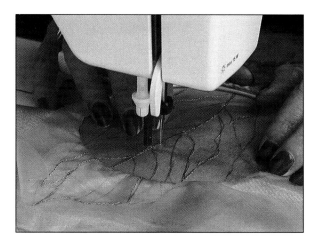

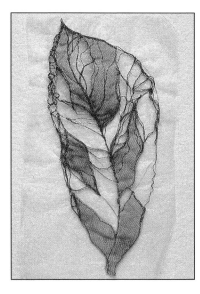

Above, right: working the main lines of the motif through the dissolvable fabric and the silk.

Above: Here the silk has been cut away in several places, leaving only the soluble material.

Right: Additional lines have been worked to link the silk areas and provide an interesting network of lines. The completed leaf is shown along with the skeletonized natural leaf that inspired it.

JEWELLERY *and* ORNAMENTS

The art of making jewellery goes back to very ancient times; in some societies it pre-dates the wearing of clothes. For primitive peoples, as for civilized ones, jewellery has traditionally been a way of displaying wealth, as well as adorning one's body.

Like other crafts, jewellery-making is strongly influenced by the materials available. Although precious jewellery uses materials, such as gems, pearls and gold, that may be obtained from far-off places, simpler ethnic jewellery tends to rely on local materials — shells, pebbles, wood and clay, for example. Today costume jewellery is increasingly popular; and stylish, elegant and witty pieces are made from glass, plastic and other synthetic, inexpensive materials.

Many embroiderers are now discovering that

Above: a design for a necklace to be made of glittery fabric shapes, based on motifs found on a mummy case.

Right: This colourful glazed paste jewellery from ancient Egypt was intended for everyday occasions. Its simple fruit and flower shapes could easily be interpreted in textile jewellery.

fabrics and threads, too, can be used to make beautiful jewellery and other three-dimensional ornaments. Machine embroidery is especially well suited to textile jewellery, because of its delicacy and strength, and I have used it for most of the items described in this section. Almost any fabrics can be used, but lightweight silk and fine, sheer fabrics such as net and organza lend themselves most readily to this work. Fine machine embroidery threads, especially metallic ones, and lustrous silk embroidery threads are most appropriate. Liquid fabric paints can be used to give fabrics interestingly 'marbled' patterns.

Before you embark on making your own textile jewellery, it is well worthwhile spending some time in museums, studying and sketching examples of jewellery from earlier times. Egyptian jewellery is a particularly fruitful source of inspiration. Then spend some time experimenting with colour schemes and different techniques, so that you acquire a feeling for the scale of different pieces of jewellery. You may wish to begin with slightly larger-scale work, such as the flowers shown on pages 130–131, which use techniques common to textile jewellery but in more easily manageable sizes.

Textile jewellery is still a new concept, but I feel that it has great potential, not only as a means of coordinating clothing and accessories but also in its own right, as an art form.

Below: another design for a necklace based on Egyptian motifs.

Bottom: Gold and semi-precious stones have been used for this ancient Egyptian jewellery.

MAKING FABRIC BEADS

Traditionally, most necklaces have been constructed of beads, of one kind or another, usually threaded onto strong thread or cord. There are several ways of making fabric beads, which can be assembled into necklaces on their own or combined with commercially made beads. Fabric beads are easy to make by hand or machine, and although the hand method is time-consuming, you will find it an activity that you can pick up at odd moments as time permits. For all the examples shown, I have used a medium-weight silk, painted with liquid paints. The silk always gives subtle, attractive colours.

METHOD 1   This method produces large beads and requires the least sewing. Like the method that follows, this one uses bought tissue balls or cotton moulds, which are usually available in a variety of sizes from necklace-makers' suppliers and craft shops.

1. Cut a length of silk long enough to cover all the beads, allowing for it to be gathered up slightly. A measurement of 40 by 8 cm (16 by 3 inches) should be suitable for 12 beads, measuring 20 mm (¾ inch) in diameter.
2. Fold the fabric lengthwise with right sides together, and stitch the long edges with a 1-cm (⅜-inch) seam.

Left: materials and techniques required for methods 1 and 2. At upper left (1), the fabric has been turned back to mark the width of the strip to be cut. Next to it, some tissue balls have been inserted and are being held in place with stitching. At lower right (2): paper templates and fabric circles, a bead in the process of being covered and a partially completed necklace made from individual fabric and purchased beads.

Opposite: materials and techniques for methods 3 and 4. At left (3): templates and circles for Suffolk puffs, along with several completed puffs. At right (4): cylindrical polyester-filled beads.

3. Turn the tube right side out, then insert tissue balls along the length. After each bead is inserted, wind a decorative embroidery thread tightly around the fabric, close to the bead, using a needle to start and finish off, so that it is fastened securely. Alternatively, the fabric beads can be interspersed with purchased beads (with large holes), threaded onto the tube after each tissue ball is inserted.

METHOD 2   This involves covering separate tissue balls with fine fabric. The beads can be assembled on a fine cord and interspersed with a variety of purchased beads.

1. Cut a circle of fabric large enough to just cover a tissue ball with the raw edge of the fabric turned in. The following is a guide to the size required: 20-mm (¾-inch) ball — 5.5-cm (2¼-inch) circle; 25-mm (1-inch) ball — 8-cm (3-inch) circle. Once you have determined the size, make a paper template to use as a pattern for all the beads.

2. Turning in the raw edge of the fabric as you go, work tiny running stitches around the edge, close to the fold. Leave the needle on the thread, place the tissue ball on the circle, and pull up the gathers. Secure the thread with a few stitches, which will help to smooth any puckers.

METHOD 3   Suffolk puffs, often used in patchwork, can also be used to make soft fabric beads.

1. Cut a circle of fabric twice the required diameter of the finished circle. Turn in the raw edge, and gather it up so that the sides turn into the middle; fasten off with a few stitches.
2. Thread the puffs onto a fine cord, interspersing them with other kinds of beads for the most attractive results. Individual Suffolk puffs can also be used for earrings.

METHOD 4 These beads are made as separate cylinders and stuffed with polyester filling.

1. Cut a piece of silk into rectangles measuring 8 by 6.5 cm (3 by 2½ inches). Fold each in half widthwise, and stitch 1 cm (⅜ inch) from the raw edges.
2. Turn the little tubes right side out. Turn in both remaining raw edges, and work running stitches through both edges, leaving the needles on the thread.
3. Push some filling into the cylinder, and gather up both ends. Fasten the ends securely, leaving a tiny gap for ease in threading the beads.

METHOD 5 This is basically the same method as that often used by children to make paper beads. I have adapted it by bonding two fabrics together and machine stitching the edges for a firm finish.

1. Mark long triangles — about 26 cm (10 inches) long and 2.5 cm (1 inch) at the base — on the paper side of transfer adhesive (fusing web). Iron the triangles onto one piece of fabric, then cut out the triangle shapes. Peel off the backing paper, then iron the shapes onto another fabric.
2. Set the machine to a narrow zigzag stitch, and work over the raw edges of the sides of the triangles.
3. Spread fabric glue thinly onto the fabric that is to be inside, leaving about 1 cm (½ inch) unglued at the base, and roll the fabric round a fine knitting needle, starting with the base of the triangle. Take care to keep the bead symmetrical.
4. When the glue has set, the beads can be slid off the needle and used on their own or along with other beads.

Left: materials and techniques for Method 5. Slender triangles have been marked onto the transfer adhesive. Two contrasting fabrics are shown bonded together and zigzag stitched along the edges. The triangle is wound onto a knitting needle as shown to form the beads.

Right: a selection of yarns, cords and fabric strips suitable for use as machine-made cords.

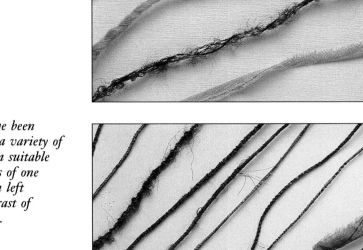

Right: cords that have been zigzag stitched with a variety of threads to make them suitable for jewellery. Sections of one fabric strip have been left unstitched for a contrast of thickness and texture.

MACHINE-MADE CORDS

Some successful jewellery can be made by combining machine-made cords with hand-made and purchased beads. It is a good idea to study pictures or examples of jewellery in order to get ideas for designs and to jot down the embroidery techniques that could be used to get the right effect. Many ancient necklaces and belts consisted of silver or gold wires twisted together, with ornaments either attached between the wires or hanging from them. We can achieve a similar effect by making our own cords from a variety of different threads and strips of fabric.

To become familiar with this technique, choose threads of various thicknesses: metallic crochet yarn, chunky knitting yarn, string of different weights and the cord used for Venetian blinds. The only restriction on the thickness of the thread used is the width of the zigzag on the machine; the core thread must be covered by stitching.

Make several cords using different threads and densities of stitching. Some lovely cords can be made by using different combinations of bobbin and top sewing threads, with a variety of core threads, including strips of fabric, decorative tapes and ribbon, and alternating blocks of stitching with un-stitched lengths.

METHOD
1. Set the machine for zigzag stitching. The width will depend on the size of thread used, and the length can be varied depending on how much of the core thread you wish to show. Choose a foot that has a groove underneath; this will prevent the cord from becoming flattened.
2. Place the thread under the foot, and work zigzag stitch over it, supporting the cord both behind and in front of the foot. This will be necessary because the cord is too narrow to be fed through by the feed dog.

MAKING NECKLACES AND BELTS FROM CORDS

The narrow cords you make by machine can be combined and used in various ways, either on their own or in conjunction with purchased cords, ribbons, and lengths of threaded beads. First assemble as large a variety of cords as possible, and try several samples before deciding on a necklace from one method.

METHOD 1: TWISTED CORDS
1. Take several cords three times the required finished length; include some purchased cords or narrow ribbons to give a variety of texture.
2. Tie the strands together at one end, and loop the knot over a convenient hook. Knot the other ends around a pencil. Turn the pencil round and round to twist the strands together very tightly; they must kink up automatically when the tension is slackened.
3. Fold the cords in half so that they twist themselves around each other to make a chunky twisted cord.

For a belt, the ends of the cord can be knotted together and the strands trimmed to make tassels. Alternately, the ends can be attached to a purchased buckle.

To make a necklace, bind the ends of the twisted cord before attaching them to a clasp. To make a really neat finish, glue the ends into a conical bell cap, available where jewellery findings are sold. Beads can be added to the necklace by threading them onto one or more of the individual cords before twisting, then repositioning them if necessary. Or they can be sewn on afterwards where desired.

METHOD 2: WRAPPING Any combination of threads, with or without beads threaded onto them, can be joined together by wrapping them at intervals by hand or machine.
For machine wrapping, set the machine to the widest zigzag, and join together all the cords in a bunch. They may need to be stitched over several times in order to be held securely.

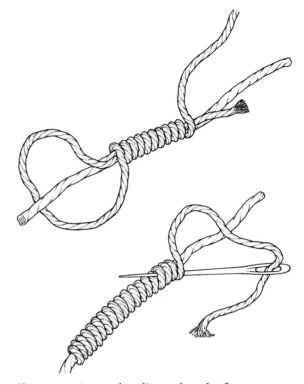

Above: starting and ending a length of hand-wrapped cord. The loop is first secured by wrapping the thread several times around it; then the short end is pulled, so that the loop disappears, leaving a neat, secure end. The remaining end is sewn into the work.

For hand wrapping, bind the strands together, either with a decorative embroidery thread or with a very narrow machine-made cord.

1. Fold over about 2.5 cm (1 inch) of the wrapping thread, and lay the loop alongside the cords to be wrapped. Holding all the threads together between thumb and forefinger, start to wrap the long end around all the threads.
2. After a few winds, pull on the short end; the loop will disappear, and the end can be cut off.
3. When the desired length of wrapping is reached, thread a large-eyed needle onto the wrapping thread. Pass this back into the work, then pull it tight and cut off the end.

Opposite: necklaces made from cords and a variety of purchased beads.

ASSEMBLING NECKLACES FROM BEADS

Most hand-made beads look better when combined with purchased ones. A contrast of scale, shape and texture is needed to give the best effect. If your beads are round, they will look better separated by flat, disc-shaped beads; flat Suffolk puff beads will need a more cylindrical shape between them.

Before making a final decision about the arrangement of the beads in the necklace, it is a good idea to experiment with different sequences to see what will look best. This can be done most easily on a grooved surface, such as a small rubber car mat or the groove in the middle of a metal ruler, which will prevent the beads from rolling around.

The largest beads should go in the middle of the necklace; the smaller ones can be arranged to go around the back of the neck. A length of about 45 cm (18 inches) makes an attractive necklace. Your choice of thread or cord will be governed by the size of the hole in the smallest bead.

METHOD 1 This is a very old method of necklace making and will suit the smallest of beads.

1. Cut a length of thread, which can be polyester buttonhole twist or medium thickness pure silk, allowing twice the length of the finished necklace plus at least 30 cm (12 inches).
2. Make a needle from an 8-cm (3-inch) length of brass wire, folded in half. (A made needle is generally most satisfactory, as it will accommodate a fairly thick thread, yet is fine enough to go through small beads.) Twist the wire at the centre to form a large eye, insert the thread, then tighten the eye with tweezers and continue twisting the wires down their length. Trim the ends with wire cutters to make a point, following the twist of the wire.
3. Pull the thread ends even to make a double strand, and tie them in a loose knot, 15 cm (6 inches) from the end.
4. Thread the beads onto the wire needle according to your planned arrangement.

Left: these necklaces show how fabric beads are complemented and enhanced by changes of scale, shape and texture, which can usually be provided by purchased beads.

Opposite: These necklaces illustrate the varied effects possible in textile jewellery. The one at top left is based on the design shown on page 116.

Left: Method 1 of assembling a necklace. Note the twisted wire needle, which is easily threaded yet will slip through small beads. Here the needle is about to be taken back through the coil to attach the clasp. The knotted ends are then trimmed close to the beads.

5. When all the beads are threaded, attach a clasp. This can be a screw clasp, for example, or a set consisting of a jump ring and a bolt ring — both sold at bead and jewellery-makers' shops.

6. Before attaching the clasp, thread a short length (5 mm [¼ inch]) of metallic purl (a fine coil of wire used in metal thread embroidery) onto the needle. This will prevent the thread from being cut by the end bead.

7. Thread one end of the clasp over the purl, then take the needle back down the hole of the first bead. Make a slip knot between the first and second beads, then take the needle through the second bead. Cut the thread to remove the needle, and knot the two threads between the second and third beads. Apply a spot of glue to both knots, squeeze them with fine-pointed tweezers, then cut off the loose ends.

8. Repeat steps 6 and 7 for the other end, starting by untying the loose knot then threading both ends of the thread through the needle.

METHOD 2 Beads with large holes can be threaded onto a much thicker thread or cord. A needle is not usually necessary; simply wind a piece of sticky tape around the end of the cord to make a firm point. Suitable types of cord include those sold for soft furnishings, leather thonging and machine-made cords (see page 121).

1. Cut a length of cord the finished length of the necklace plus at least 33 cm (13 inches).
2. Thread the beads onto the cords. Make sure that they are centred, then knot the cord at the end of the beads to prevent them from moving. If necessary, tie a small knot at each end of the cord to prevent fraying. The necklace can then simply be tied around the neck.

EARRINGS

By using a combination of any of the techniques described in this chapter, you can make some very pretty and wearable earrings. However, you should study the sizes and shapes of purchased earrings before becoming too carried away with the idea; without careful attention to scale, the results might look better on a Christmas tree than adorning someone's ear!

Any of the bead-making techniques will be suitable, especially when combined with purchased beads and machine-made cords. Separate motifs, such as geometric shapes or flowers, can be hung from a small cord or a wire ring. The shapes can be made from scraps of fabric, either machine-stitched around the edge, sandwiched between sheer fabrics or mounted onto soluble fabric (as described for 'Fabric flowers', page 130). Shapes cut from cardboard or wood can easily be covered with threads in colourful geometric patterns.

Try all of the following methods, using different fabrics and threads, and study examples of ethnic jewellery for design ideas. You might even discover new techniques for making earrings.

WRAPPED CARDBOARD This is a very simple method which involves no sewing. Shiny and metallic threads are especially effective.

1. Cut some small triangles of cardboard. A good size has a base measuring 2.5 cm (1 inch) and sides of 3.5 cm (1½ inches).
2. Cover both sides of each triangle with double-sided tape; trim the edges of the tape even with the cardboard.

Below: assembling a bead earring (see page 128). The thread is taken back through the bead to secure it.

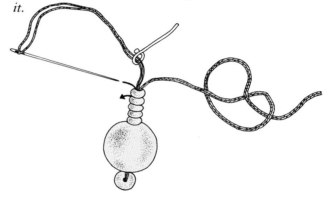

Left: These graceful earrings, by Annwyn Dean, are made from Suffolk puffs, purchased wires and tiny beads.

Left: Cardboard shapes and wooden cubes have been wrapped with various shiny and fuzzy threads to make these dangling earrings.

Opposite: a variety of shapes, some worked on soluble fabric, have been used to make these earrings. At upper left, a shape has been pinned to some soluble fabric, prior to working a lacy edge, as on the completed earring below it.

3. Beginning at the base, and holding the short end in place until it is held secure by the wrapping, cover the triangle with the threads. Peel away the paper of the double-sided tape as wrapping proceeds. Several different threads can be incorporated into each triangle.

4. At the point, apply a spot of glue to secure the end of the thread. With a stiletto, make a hole through the threads and cardboard about 5 mm (¼ inch) in from the point of the triangle. Thread a circular earring wire through the hole.

A similar method can be used with small cubes of soft wood, such as balsa, which are wrapped with threads in both directions. These can be suspended by a thread, secured under the wrapped threads and then threaded with small beads, or by means of a long silver wire called a head-pin, which is attached to the earring finding by bending the end into a hook with a pair of pliers.

BEAD EARRINGS   For this method, first experiment with a selection of your hand-made beads, mixing them with purchased beads for the best effect. It is important for the earrings to hang freely, so the purchased beads will be helpful in adding the necessary weight.

1. Thread a wire needle (see page 124) with medium-thickness silk thread; tie a loose knot about 13 cm (6 inches) from one end.

2. Thread several purchased beads onto the thread, pass the needle through the middle of the hand-made bead, through one more purchased bead, then back through the remaining beads.

3. Loop the needle end over the ring of the earring finding, take it back through the first bead, then knot and fasten off. Re-thread the needle onto the spare end, then take it back through two beads before knotting and fastening off. The knots can be fixed with a spot of glue, then squeezed with fine tweezers to seal the ends.

FLAT AND MOULDED SHAPES   There are many ways of making individual shapes suitable for earrings (and for other pieces of jewellery). Any of the methods shown on page 130 can be used, and the resulting motifs hung singly or in clusters from a machine-wrapped cord. Tiny beads or sequins can be added to give a more jewel-like effect.
Flower and leaf shapes can be made by simply outlining in free machine stitching. If the fabrics do not seem substantial enough, they can be used

double. Geometric shapes, such as squares, circles and rectangles, can be made in essentially the same way, by outlining the edges in satin stitch, with the foot on the machine.

More complex motifs can be achieved using several layers of fabric. For ideas, look at ethnic jewellery, which is often incised or painted in interesting patterns. The designs will need to be simplified for earrings, because of the tiny scale, but an effective result can be achieved by superimposing several layers of thin fabric, stitching simple shapes in free machine embroidery, then cutting back some of the layers to reveal the different fabrics.

Shapes with lacy edges can be created using Method 3 for fabric flowers, described on page 130. Beads or sequins can be added for extra sparkle, and the shape suspended from a beaded or machine-wrapped cord.

Spiralling shapes can be made following Method 5 for fabric beads, described on page 120; cut the triangles to measure about 10 by 1.5 cm (4 by ⅝ inches), and when zigzag stitching the long sides, work over a length of fine wire, pinched into a small loop at the apex of the triangle. Mould the triangle diagonally over a thick knitting needle to form a spiral, and slide the loop over a wire earring finding.

Above: earrings made from various textile and purchased beads.

FABRIC FLOWERS

Beautiful flowers, which can be used for hair ornaments, corsages and floral arrangements, can easily be made from fabric, using a variety of hand and machine techniques. The fabrics may be sheer or opaque, but should be lightweight. Fabric paints can be applied to them to create subtle colourings. The flower and leaf shapes can be imaginary or based on real ones.

LEAF AND FLOWER SHAPES — METHOD 1   For this simple method the machine is used with the presser foot on.

1. Make a paper pattern of the shape required; this can be traced from a book or gardening catalogue.
2. Place two pieces of fabric together with wrong sides facing, and pin the pattern on top.
3. Machine stitch around the edge of the pattern, using a straight stitch and leaving the presser foot on. You may wish to leave a small gap for inserting the stem.
4. Remove the paper shape, tearing it away gently if caught by the stitching. Cut close to the stitching with sharp scissors.

5. Work satin stitch over the edge, covering the straight stitching, to prevent fraying. (Avoid making the stitch too wide and solid, which produces a heavy effect.)

METHOD 2   This method uses water-soluble fabric (see page 112). Make several different shapes, using a variety of threads to mix and coordinate the colours.

1. Either pin a paper pattern onto the fabric or trace the design through the fabric with a soft pencil.
2. Work free machine embroidery onto the soluble fabric, making sure that all lines of stitching are linked. If you include a metallic thread either in the bobbin or as the top thread, the shape will hold together more firmly after the fabric has been dissolved.

METHOD 3   This method also uses the soluble fabric, but incorporates a piece of woven fabric. It gives much firmer shapes than Method 2. They are also quicker to make, as they require less stitching.

1. Cut the woven fabric to the desired size and shape.

Left: These hand-wrapped wires, leaves and flower shapes, some worked on soluble fabric, can be used to make hair ornaments, bouquets and other accessories.

Opposite: a bouquet of fabric flowers, tied with narrow ribbon and placed in a pretty glass vase, makes an attractive ornament.

2. Tack (baste) the fabric shape to the framed-up soluble fabric.
3. Stitch the design lines through both fabrics, running off the edge of the shape to make a lacy edge.

MAKING STEMS – METHOD 1   This method of hand wrapping can be done with a perle cotton for a shiny finish or with a knitting yarn for a soft, fuzzy texture.

1. Cut pieces of plastic-covered garden wire slightly longer than the required length.
2. Cut a length of thread at least three times as long as the wire. Fold over one end to form a loop about 4 cm (1½ inches) long, and lay this along one end of the wire (see drawing, page 122). Start winding the long end of thread over the wire and the loop, leaving part of the loop showing. When about 1 cm (½ inch) has been wrapped, pull on the short end until the

loop disappears. Cut off the short end of thread and the exposed wire.

3. Continue wrapping to the other end. Finish off by threading the free end back up under the wrapping with a needle. If this proves difficult, a spot of glue can be used to seal the cut end.

METHOD 2 – MACHINE WRAPPING

1. With the presser foot on the machine, set the controls for a wide, short zigzag stitch.
2. Place the wire under the middle of the foot, and supporting it both in front and behind, work satin stitch over it. The machine controls may need adjusting in order for the stitching to cover the wire; or, if necessary, the wire can be fed through the machine a second time. The wire will still need supporting, as the feed dog teeth will be ineffective in pushing it through.

Above: This exquisite bridal headdress by Sylvia Dymant is made entirely of fabric flowers, embellished with tiny pearl beads.

ASSEMBLING THE FLOWERS The wires can be joined to the flowers and leaves by oversewing (overcasting). If there are two layers of fabric, the stem can be gently slid between the layers and sewn in place. If the stitching shows, it can be concealed by applying a few beads or sequins.

Two or more flower shapes can be superimposed and sewn together in the centre to make more three-dimensional blossoms. For a corsage, simply gather the stems together and tie them with embroidery thread or narrow ribbons. For a hair ornament, leave part of the stems unwrapped, so that they can be wound onto a comb or other base, which can then be partially covered with ribbon. Stems can also be left partly unwrapped for floral arrangements, and inserted in a block of Oasis flower arranging foam.

Practical Information

USING A FRAME

The three main types of embroidery frame are described on page 25. The method of mounting the fabric in these frames is described below.

ROUND FRAMES   If the area to be worked is larger than the frame, so that the frame will have to be moved, you should first bind one of the rings with bias tape or seam binding, in order to protect the work from possible snagging and to help the frame grip the fabric. Bind the outer ring if working hand stitchery, the inner ring for machine work, as these are the surfaces that will touch the right side of the fabric in each case. If the work will be highly textured, a ring frame should not be used, as it will crush the stitches.

1. Adjust the screw so that the outer ring fits snugly, but not tightly, over the inner one.
2. Separate the rings and place the fabric over the inner ring.
3. Press the outer ring over it, applying pressure as evenly as possible so as not to distort the fabric. The grain of the fabric should be straight and the fabric very taut. If necessary, remove the outer ring, adjust the screw and try again.

RECTANGULAR FRAMES   The fabric should be cut slightly larger than the frame, and if it is soft or loosely woven, it should first be backed with a firmer, though lightweight, fabric. Tack (baste) the fabrics together through the centre in both directions.

1. Mark the centre of each side of the fabric. The centre of each side of the frame should be marked also.

2. Attach the fabric to the frame on one side, using a drawing pin (thumbtack) or a staple and matching the centre points.
3. Attach it at the opposite centre point, pulling the fabric taut.
4. Repeat steps 2 and 3 on the other two sides. Continue in this way, working outward from the centres and on alternate sides, so that the grain of the fabric is straight and the fabric taut. The drawing pins should be placed about 2.5 cm (1 inch) apart.

SLATE FRAMES   If you are working a piece of embroidery smaller than the frame, first mount it on a larger piece of fabric. The embroidery can then be worked through both layers. The method of mounting the fabric on this kind of frame is called 'dressing' the frame. (The method described below, and illustrated on page 134, applies to the type of frame shown on page 25.)

Begin with the frame separated into its four parts.

1. Press under a 2-cm (¾-inch) hem on the top and bottom edges and then on the side edges of the fabric.
2. Cut two generous lengths of string. Slip one under each side hem and machine stitch the hem in place, thus forming a casing. The purpose of these strings is to provide a firm edge for the lacing.
3. Mark the centre of the other edges and the centre of the webbing strips. Match these points and sew the fabric to the webbing with oversewing (overcasting).
4. Slot the laths through the rollers, and fix them at the correct distance with the pegs provided.
5. Thread a large-eyed needle with some string, about four–five times the length of the side.

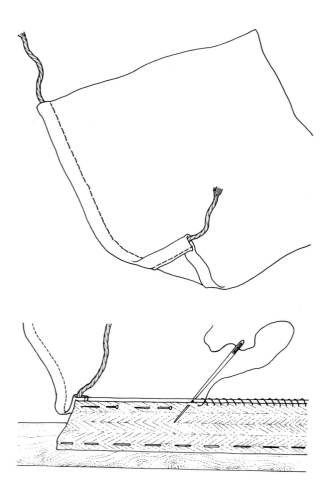

Tie the string securely to the frame, then lace the fabric to the laths as shown, working over the string and placing the stitches about 3 cm (1¼ inches) apart. Repeat on the other side.

6. Pull up the lacing strings along their entire length so that the fabric is taut, and tie them to the lower corners of the frame.

WORKING WITH A FRAME   When working embroidery in a frame, you will need to use stabbing — rather than sewing — movements with the needle, working with both hands and keeping one hand under the work. However, you may prefer to work looped stitches, such as fly or buttonhole, with a sewing movement; and for this the fabric will need to be slackened off in the frame. This can be done fairly easily with a ring frame or a slate frame (on which you can loosen the lacing strings), but if you are using a rectangular frame, you should consider this at the outset and mount the fabric accordingly.

DAMP-STRETCHING

After all the time and effort you have spent working a piece of embroidery, it is well worthwhile spending a little more time to ensure that the work is presented in an attractive and professional manner. Even if the embroidery was worked on a frame, it will need to be damp-stretched in order to restore the natural grain of the background fabric, which may have become puckered by stitching. Never attempt to iron embroidery, for the threads will be flattened and lose their original textural qualities.

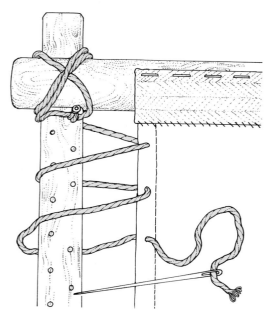

1. Lay several sheets of newspaper on a flat wooden board.
2. Slowly pour over the newspaper enough water to soak it thoroughly.
3. Cover the wet newspaper with at least two thicknesses of absorbent white paper; either blotting paper or kitchen paper towel is suitable.
4. Lay the piece of embroidery *right* side up on the white paper. Pin the fabric to shape with drawing pins (thumbtacks), starting at the centres and working outwards and checking frequently with a ruler to make sure that the

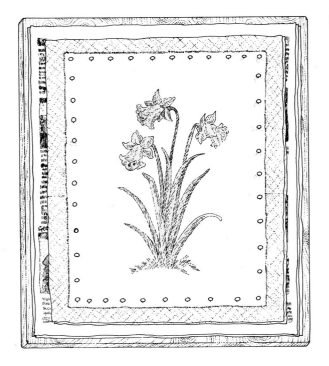

Damp-stretching the completed embroidery.

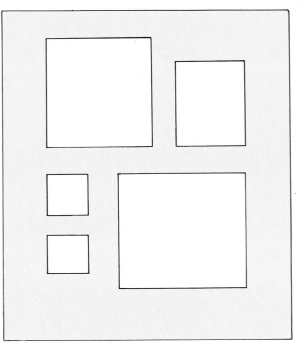

A card mount for displaying several pieces of work.

sides are straight and the corners true right angles.

5. Leave the work undisturbed until the newspaper has dried, which in a damp climate may take up to two days. The embroidery will now be completely flat and ready for mounting and framing.

MOUNTING

There are several methods of presenting a finished piece of embroidery. The choice in a given case will depend on such factors as the size of the piece, where it is to be hung and whether or not glass is required. For very small samples of embroidery it is convenient to use a simple card mount (mat). Depending on size, this can accommodate one or more samples. The mounted work can then be placed in a picture frame, if desired.

Opposite: steps in mounting fabric on a slate frame. The string in the casing provides a firm edge for the lacing, which holds the fabric taut.

CARD MOUNTS (MATS)
1. To make a single card mount (mat), first determine the size of the window and the overall size of the mount.
2. Subtract the smaller depth and width measurements from the larger ones to find out how much will be left for margins; these should be the same at the sides and top and slightly greater at the lower edge.
3. Mark the window on the back of a piece of mounting (mat) board, and cut, using a strong craft knife and a metal ruler with an indented groove to protect the fingers. Press the knife firmly into the corners, then along the length of each side. With experience, you will find it neater to cut the mounts from the front, but initially it is much easier to mark and cut from the back of the board.
4. Fix the piece of embroidery to the back of the mount with masking tape.

When combining several small samples of embroidery in one mount, it is worthwhile cutting out pieces of paper the correct size and arranging these on the mounting (mat) board before measuring or cutting. The same rule regarding the width of the margins at the sides applies, but the measurement will apply only to the edges of the two pieces that are nearest the sides of the mount. When mounting several shapes, it is important to consider their relationship with each other and not to allow them to have awkward spaces between them. I usually start near the middle of the board with the larger shapes, then work towards the edges with the smaller ones. The lower margin of the mount must still be deeper than the sides and top, in order to avoid creating the optical illusion of its appearing smaller.

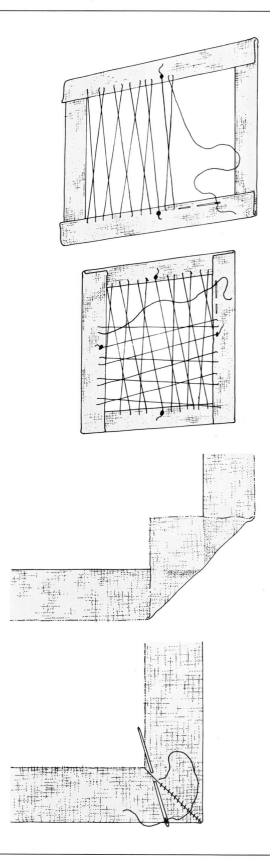

LACING Medium-sized pieces of embroidery, intended to be hung individually, should be laced to a firm backing to keep them smooth.

1. Cut a piece of thick cardboard or hardboard to the exact size of the finished embroidery. If the work is to be inserted in a frame, the cardboard needs to be cut slightly larger.
2. Trim the embroidery fabric to approximately 2.5 cm (1 inch) larger than the cardboard all around. Place it face down and lay the cardboard on top.
3. Turn the edges of the fabric over the cardboard, and hold them in place temporarily with masking tape. If the fabric is bulky or if the corners will be visible, it is necessary to mitre the corners, as described below.
4. Lace the fabric edges together, first vertically then horizontally, using strong thread and herringbone stitch. Start in the middle and work outwards to one side then the other.

To mitre corners, fold the corner in diagonally and glue it in place; then fold the adjacent sides in to meet each other. Pin or tack (baste) them in place, then slipstitch the folded edges together.
For a slightly padded effect, glue a piece of thin wadding (batting) to the cardboard before covering it.
The work can now be put into a picture frame or double-mounted onto another piece of fabric-covered board. If neither of these treatments is used, the back will need to be covered with a piece

of fabric, which is slipstitched to the embroidery fabric.

Larger pieces of work can be stretched over hardboard and attached to it on the back with masking tape without lacing. The corners will still need to be mitred, as described above, if the fabric is bulky. So long as the work has been thoroughly stretched beforehand, this is a very satisfactory method of mounting the work.

FRAMING WITHOUT A FRAME

In some situations a conventional wooden or metal frame would be an unsuitable treatment for an embroidered panel. Here are some simple but attractive alternatives.

MOUNTING ONTO FABRIC A fabric surround makes a sympathetic finish for a piece of embroidery, especially if the fabric is chosen carefully so that it complements the work. It should pick up one of the colours in the embroidery; with a subtle application of fabric paints, you could pick up several of the colours. If choosing a solid-coloured fabric, select an appropriate texture; for example, velvet may complement highly textured stitchery.

There are two basic methods of applying the embroidery to fabric:

Double mounting   In this method, the embroidery is first laced or glued to a piece of thick cardboard, as described on page 136.

1. Cut a piece of hardboard to the required finished size of the work.
2. Cover it with the chosen fabric, gluing or lacing it in place.
3. Slipstitch the panel to the fabric background using a curved upholsterer's needle, This will be somewhat easier if the large board has been padded with a piece of thin wadding (batting).

Machine stitching:
1. Machine stitch the embroidery to the background fabric.
2. Trim the work close to the stitching and fray the raw edges.

GLASS CLIP FRAMES   If the embroidery is quite flat, with little surface texture, it can be attractively presented — and protected from dust — in a glass clip frame. This type of frame, often used for photographs, is available in a wide range of sizes. Instead of a conventional moulding, metal clips hold the glass in place.

1. Choose a frame larger than the embroidery. The frame should have a black or white mounting (mat) board, but you may prefer to cut your own in an appropriate colour.
2. Neaten the edges of the embroidery with machine stitching; trim close to the edge and then fray it.
3. Attach the work to the card with double-sided tape. Assemble the layers and clip them together.

FABRIC FRAMES

An interesting way of presenting a piece of embroidery is to make a fabric-covered frame, embroidered so as to co-ordinate with the main work. The technique is particularly suitable for subjects such as a view through a window or doorway or part of a landscape 'framed' by foliage. The embroidery on the frame can either continue the design from within the frame or change the scale by being worked in a different embroidery technique. An example of this device is shown below; another can be found on page 13.

The basic method of making a fabric frame, described below, will have to be adapted to suit the embroidery technique being used; but in all cases the embroidery is completed before the frame is made up.

1. Cut a cardboard frame of the required size; cut another piece of cardboard the same size to serve as the backing.
2. Cut the fabric approximately 2 cm (¾ inch) larger than the frame on all sides. Also cut out a piece of 4 oz (extra-loft) wadding (batting) just slightly larger than the frame.
3. Place the fabric face down and lay the wadding and frame on top. Turn the outer corners diagonally over the frame, and secure them with a piece of masking tape. Stick the outer side edges in place with fabric glue.
4. Mitre the outer corners by slipstitching the diagonal seams, as shown on page 136, to make the corners square.
5. Carefully clip the inner corners of the fabric almost to the corner of the frame. Turn the

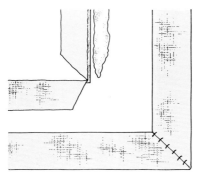

Left: a quilted fabric frame makes an appropriate surround for a small piece of stitchery. Continuing the embroidery onto the frame achieves an integrated effect.

inner edges over the frame and fasten them with fabric glue.

6. Apply the piece of embroidery to the other piece of cardboard with fabric glue or double-sided tape.

7. Place the frame over the embroidery, and secure it with fabric glue. Or, for a stronger and neater finish, first cover the back of the mounted embroidery with fabric, covering the edges, then slipstitch this to the back of the frame.

In the example shown, which depicts cosmos flowers in a garden, the embroidered picture was worked, then carefully aligned with the cut-out piece of frame fabric to establish the position of the additional embroidery to be worked on the frame. The effect of a wall was achieved by machine quilting.

MAKING A CUSHION COVER

Cushions are among the most popular of embroidered items, lending themselves to all sorts of techniques, including appliqué and hand stitchery. Making up a simple cushion cover is not difficult; however, if you wish to insert a zip fastener to make the cover removable, or to finish the seams with thick cord, you may prefer to have the making-up done professionally. Some books on soft furnishings give instructions for these more complex techniques.

1. For the back of the cover cut a piece of fabric the same size as the front. Both pieces should measure 2 cm (¾ inch) larger all around than the size of the finished cover. If quilting is the technique used for the front cover, it is a good idea to include a thin layer of wadding (batting) for the back also, to give it body. This can be tacked (basted) to the wrong side of the fabric outside the seam allowance.

2. Place the two pieces of fabric together with right sides facing. Tack (baste) and stitch them together, taking 2 cm (¾ inch) seam allowance and leaving a gap approximately 25 cm (10 inches) long in one side.

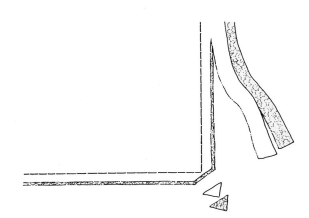

3. Trim the seam allowances and cut across the corners diagonally to reduce bulk. Press the seam open, and zigzag stitch or oversew (overcast) the edges to prevent fraying.

4. Turn the cover right side out, and insert the cushion pad (pillow form). Close the gap with slipstitching.

FOR A NARROW PIPED EDGE:
1. Cut a length of narrow piping cord to go around all edges, plus about 10 cm (4 inches) extra.

2. Cut a bias strip of fabric the same length, wide enough to go around the cord plus 4 cm (1½ inches); wrap this around the cord and stitch close to it, using the zipper foot.

3. Tack (baste) the piping to the right side of the back cover piece, with the raw edges even, overlapping the ends as shown. Stitch it in place.

4. Make up the cover as described above, steps 2–4.

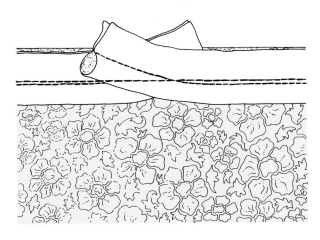

SUPPLIERS

Most art and design materials can be purchased from a good art shop; fabrics and threads, from specialist needlecraft shops. These are well advertised, in Britain, in craft magazines – particularly *Embroidery* magazine (published quarterly by the Embroiderers' Guild and available from E.G. Enterprises Ltd., P.O. Box 42B, East Molesey, Surrey KT8 9BB) and *Crafts* magazine (published every two months by The Crafts Council, 8 Waterloo Place, London SW1Y 4AT). In other countries, the local Yellow Pages are generally the most useful source of suppliers' addresses, although needlecraft magazines are also well worth investigating.

IN GREAT BRITAIN

Borovicks
16 Berwick Street
London W1
The theatrical department is an Aladdin's cave of exotic organzas, brocades, silks, satins and metallic fabrics.

Creative Beadcraft Ltd
Denmark Works
Sheepcote Dell Road
Beaumond End
Amersham
Bucks HP7 0RX
Mail order or personal callers. This is the mail order department of Ells & Farrier Ltd, and supplies beads, tissue balls and jewellery findings.

Dunlicraft Ltd
Pullman Road
Wigston
Leicester LE8 2DY
Main suppliers of DMC threads. Write for information and lists of stockists.

Ells and Farrier Ltd
20 Princes Street
Hanover Square
London W1 8PH
Personal callers only. Beads, sequins, tissue balls, jewellery findings.

John Lewis
Oxford Street
London W1
Branches in many large towns supplying haberdashery (notions), furnishing and dress fabrics, fabric paints.

Liberty & Co
Regent Street
London W1
Unusual fabrics, knitting yarns, embroidery supplies.

Madeira Threads (UK) Ltd
Ryder House
Back Lane
Boroughbridge
North Yorkshire YO5 9AT
Main suppliers of machine embroidery threads: cotton, rayon and metallic. Also a wide range of threads for hand stitchery. Write for information and lists of stockists.

Mulberry Silks
Unit 12A
Worcester Road Industrial Estate
Worcester Road
Chipping Norton
Oxfordshire OX7 5XW
Mail order only. Wide range of pure silk threads for hand stitching.

Shades
57 Candlemas Lane
Beaconsfield
Bucks HP9 1AE
Mail order only. Wide range of unusual and difficult-to-obtain embroidery supplies, including fabric paints and water-soluble fabric.

Silken Strands
33 Linksway
Gatley
Cheadle
Cheshire SK8 4LA
Mail order only. Machine embroidery threads.

The Bead Shop
Neal Street
London W1
Beads of all types, jewellery findings and cords.

Whaleys (Bradford) Ltd
Harris Court
Great Horton
Bradford
West Yorkshire BD7 4EQ
Wide range of fabrics, many prepared for dyeing. Minimum order 3 metres of each fabric.

George Weil & Sons Ltd
63–65 Riding House Street
London W1P 7PP
Wide range of silks and cottons suitable for fabric painting and dyeing, water-soluble fabric and fabric paints.

IN THE UNITED STATES

for design materials
Aiko's Art Materials Import Inc.
714 N. Wabash Avenue
Chicago IL 60611

Dharma Trading Co.
P.O. Box 916
San Rafael CA 94902

Farquhar International Ltd
56 Harvester Avenue
Batavia NY 14020

for threads; will provide lists of retailers
Appleton Bros. of London
West Main Road
Little Compton RI 02837

DMC Corporation
107 Trumbull Street
Elizabeth NJ 07206

Paternayan Bros. Inc.
312 East 95th Street
New York NY 10028

Susan Bates Inc.
P.O. Box E
Route 9A
212 Middlesex Avenue
Chester CO 06412

general materials
Carol's Crafts Inc.
PO Box 230
Winchester MA 01890

Elite Design
P.O. Box 894
Dalton GA 30720

Kelpar Needlecraft
P.O. Box 5177
Scottsdale AZ 85261

Stitch 'n' Stuff
24401 Carla Lane
North Olmstead OH 44070

The American Needlewoman
Box 6472
Fort Worth TX 76115

The Craft House
College Estates Station
Box 1043-B
Frederick MD 21701

Thumbelina
P.O. Box 1065
Solvang CA 93463

IN AUSTRALIA (BY REGION)

New South Wales
All Handcraft Supplies
101 Warringah Mall
Brookvale
Telephone 938 2221

Beecroft Village Craft Supplies
2 Beecroft Arcade
Beecroft
Telephone 481 0052

Hornsby Craft Centre
21 Westfield Shoppingtown
Hornsby
Telephone 476 2501

Simply Stitches
Rear 387 Victoria Avenue
Chatswood
412 4342

Victoria
Handcraft House
200 Glenferrie Road
Malvern
Telephone 509 7148

Bargello
819 Glenferrie Road
Hawthorn
Telephone 818 4853

Box Hill Art and Craft Centre
Shop 48
Whitehorse Plaza Shopping Centre
Box Hill
Telephone 890 9328

Nancraft
289 Elizabeth Street
Melbourne
Telephone 670 6221
and
246 Dorset Road
Boronia
Telephone 762 1751

Queensland
Anycraft
Shop 4, 80 City Road
Beenleigh
Telephone 287 1200

Craft Supplies Centre
120 Kingston Road
Uderwood
Telephone 208 8503

Craft World
Brookside Shopping Centre
Osborne Road
Mitchelton
Telephone 354 2454

Capalaba Park Shopping Centre
Redland Bay Road
Capalaba
Telephone 390 2791

South Australia
Cottage Crafts
462 Fullarton Road
Myrtle Bank
Telephone 79 6070

Homework
552 Milne Road
Redwood Park
Telephone 265 0238

Tracy Marsh Craft and Decorating
Centre
94 Wright Street
Adelaide
Telephone 51 4970

Western Australia
Arts and Crafts Corner
34 Mint Street
East Victoria Park
Telephone 361 4567

The Calico House
1a Glyde Street
Mosman Park
Telephone 383 3794

Knightcraft Craft Shop
25 Yampi Way
Willetton
Telephone 457 2126

With Best Wishes
339 Canning Highway
Palmyra
Telephone 339 2037

Tasmania
From Lois With Love
311 Elizabeth Street
Hobart
Telephone 34 5469

Petit Point
57 George Street
Launceston
Telephone 31 2021

Petit Point
55 Mount Street
Burnie
Telephone 31 8316

FOR FURTHER READING

The Art of the Needle, by Jan Beaney.
Century Hutchinson, London 1988

Australian Country Women's Crafts, by
The Country Women's Association.
Lloyd O'Neil Pty Limited, Melbourne
1986

Design Focus, by Hal Missingham. Van
Nostrand Reinhold, New York 1978

Design Sources for Embroidery, by Vicky
Lugg. Batsford, London 1988

Draw Flowers & Plants, by Mary
Seymour. Pitman House, London 1980

Draw Landscapes, by Norman Battershill.
Pitman House, London 1980

Drawing & Design for Embroidery, by
Richard Box. Batsford, London 1988

The Embroiderer's Garden, by Thomasina
Beck. David & Charles, Exeter 1988

The Embroiderer's Workbook, by Jan
Messent. Batsford, London 1988

Encyclopaedia of Needlework, by Therese
de Dillmont. Bracken Books, London
1987

Fabrics for Embroidery, by Jean Littlejohn.
Batsford, London 1986

Flowers & Plants in Embroidery, by Valerie
Campbell-Harding. Batsford, London
1986

Machine Appliqué Made Easy, by Jan
Brooke. Child & Associates, Sydney
1989

*Machine Embroidery: Lace and
See-Through Techniques*, by Moyra
McNeill. Batsford, London 1985

Machine Embroidery: Stitch Techniques, by
Valerie Campbell-Harding and Pam
Watts. Batsford, London 1989

Needlework School, by the Practical Study
Group of the Embroiderers' Guild.
Windward, Leicester 1984

Stitches: New Approaches, by Jan Beaney.
Batsford, London 1985

ACKNOWLEDGMENTS

I would like to thank my husband John, son Tim and daughter Kate for their constant encouragement and for their willingness to let the book, on occasion, take precedence over meals or clean clothes.

I also owe thanks to Kay Swancutt for her invaluable help with the fabric beads and earrings, to Margaret Thorpe for her encouragement and to all the people who kindly allowed me to use their work. Cara Wigham, of Dunlicraft Ltd., and Ian Mac-Pherson, of Madeira Threads (U.K.) Ltd., kindly allowed me to use their embroidery threads for the photographs, and Anne Richmond, of Elna Sewing Machines (G.B.), provided the machine.

Many thanks to Eleanor Van Zandt for her expertise with the text, to Bill Mason for the excellent design and to Stewart Grant for his inspiring photographs. My final thanks to my publishers, Merehurst Ltd. – and especially to Shirley Patton – for their support and enthusiasm for the book.

Julia Barton, Amersham, 1989

NOTE All work is by the author unless otherwise credited.

PHOTOGRAPHY ACKNOWLEDGMENTS

Page 8 Syon Cope.
By kind permission of the Victoria & Albert Museum/The Bridgeman Art Library
Page 9 (top) 'Mary Cornwallis' by George Gower.
By kind permission of Manchester City Art Galleries
(bottom) Wall hanging (*detail*).
By kind permission of Schweizerisches Landesmuseum, Zurich/The Bridgeman Art Library
Page 10 Calke Abbey state bed.
By kind permission of Country Life/the National Trust/Calke Abbey
Page 13 *All photographs by kind permission of the Crafts Council*
(top) *Photographed by Stewart Warren*
(centre) *Photographed by Stephanie Tuckwell* (bottom) *Photographed by Eleri Mills*
Page 26 Norwegian mountain scene.
Photographed by Bill Mason
Page 27 (top) Scene near Siena, Tuscany, Italy.
Photographed by Weinberg/Clark.
By kind permission of The Image Bank (bottom left) Santorini, Greece.
Photographed by Weinberg/Clark.
By kind permission of The Image Bank (bottom right) Seascape.
Photographed by Bill Mason
Page 31 Flowers and rock face.
Both photographed by Bill Mason

Page 32 Ground-covering plants and old stone wall.
Both photographed by Bill Mason
Page 35 Museum Studies.
Photographed by Bill Mason
Page 36 (left) 'La cathédrale de Rouen: harmonie blanche effet du matin', 1894
by Claude Monet.
By kind permission of The Louvre, Paris/Photographie Giraudon
(right) 'La cathédrale de Rouen: harmonie bleue, soleil matinal', 1894
by Claude Monet.
By kind permission of The Louvre, Paris/Photographie Giraudon
Page 37 'Open Window at Collioure', 1905
by Henri Matisse.
The John Hay Whitney Collection, New York.
Photo Archives Matisse (D.R.)
© *Succession Henri Matisse/DACS/ 1989*
Page 45 Fuchsias.
Photographed by Julia Barton
Page 54 Delphiniums.
Photographed by Julia Barton
Page 58 English crewel work, c.1700.
The Embroiderers' Guild Collection.
© *The Embroiderers' Guild*
Page 59 Coffin cloth in coloured wool embroidery.
By kind permission of Norsk

Folkmuseum, Oslo/The Bridgeman Art Library
Page 74 Victorian ironwork of Smithfield Market.
Photographed by Julia Barton
Page 80 English quilted waistcoat.
The Embroiderers' Guild Collection.
© *The Embroiderers' Guild*
Page 81 *Star-motif quilt reproduced by kind permission of The Patchwork Dog and the Calico Cat, London*
Page 83 'Flaneswood Morris' quilt by Julia Walker.
Photographed by Julia Walker
Page 87 Rock strata.
Photographed by Julia Barton
Page 88 Pentecost altar frontal made by the Sarum Group.
Designed by Jane Lemon.
Letters by Margaret Hague.
Frontal work by Jane Lemon and Catherine Talbot.
By kind permission of Radley College, Abingdon, Oxfordshire
Page 89 Oxburgh Hanging detail: 'A Byrd of America'.
By courtesy of the Board of Trustees of the Victoria and Albert Museum
Page 92 Pink geraniums.
Photographed by Julia Barton
Page 105 Ivy-covered house.
Photographed by Bill Mason
Pages 116–117 Egyptian jewellery.
By kind permission of The British Museum/Michael Holford Photographs

INDEX

Appliqué 75, 76, 88–93
   fabrics for 19, 88
   free 92
   hand, by 90
   machine, by 91
   three-dimensional 93
   use of 88

Background fabrics 19, *20*
Blackwork 9
Box, Richard *11*
Brushes 17
Buttonhole stitch 64, 65

Canvas work, origin of 9
Caprara, Julia *13*
Charcoal 16
Chilton, Linda *94*
Chinese embroidery
   silk 10
   wall hangings *10*
Chippindale, Jenny *34*
Coffin cloth *59*
Colonies, embroidery in 9
Colour
   analogous 40, 41
   complementary 41
   mixing 38
   schemes, looking at 42, 43
   tints, tones and shades 39
   use of 36, 37
   wheel 38, 39
Colour Sound—Garden
   Light—September 13
Coloured inks 17
Coloured papers 15
Coloured pencils 16
Coloured tissue 15
Conté crayons 16
Cords
   jewellery, used for 122, *123*
   machine-made 121
Cornwallis, Mary *9*
Cotton
   threads *22*
   use of 10
Couching 67, 100, 101
Court, Beryl *91*
Crayons
   conté 16
   transfer 18, 55

Crewel work
   origin of 9
   stitches *58*
   wool trade, stimulated by 10
Cushion cover
   making up 139
   quilted 84

Damp-stretching 134
Dean, Annwyn *90, 127*
Design
   embroidery, to 50–57
   enlarging 29, *29*
   equipment 17
   flat pattern 78, 79
   materials for 15–17
   methods 26
   repeat 78, 79
   sources of inspiration 26–35
   transfer methods 56, 57
Dobson, Rosemary *93*
Drawing
   exercises 45–48
   materials 15, 16
   subject 44
Dyes 19

Education 11
Edwards, Jean *84*
Embroiderers' Guild 11
Embroidery
   cushion cover 139
   damp-stretching 134
   frames 25, 133, 138
   framing 137
   modern materials 12
   mounting 135–137
   net 110, 111
   traditions 8–10
   transfer pencil 24
   twentieth-century 11–13
English quilting 81–83
Evenweave fabrics 20, 21
Eyelets 69, 72, 73

Fabric flowers 130–132
Fabric frame 138
Fabric markers 18, 24, 54
Fabric paints
   application of 51
   liquid 18, 52
   types of 18

   use of 12, 66
Fabrics
   appliqué, for 19, 88
   background 19, *20*
   beads, making 118–121
   design, getting onto 50
   evenweave *20, 21*
   flowers 130–132
   machine embroidery, for 95
   transparent, machine work on
      108–111
   types of 19–21
   water-soluble 112
Flaneswood Morris quilt 82
Flax, use of 10
Fly stitch 62, 63
Frame
   fabric 138
   framing without 137
   glass clip 137
   machine embroidery, for 95
   rectangular 25
   round 25, 133
   scroll 25
   slate 25, 133
   tambour 25
   types of 25
   using 133
   working with 134, *135*

Gower, George 9
Gouache paint 17
   mixing colours with 38

Home furnishings, embroidering
   8, 9
Howard, Angela *61*

In My Craft or Sullen Art 13
Italian quilting 85

Jewellery
   cords 121–123, *122*
   earrings 127–129, *127*
   fabric beads, making 118–121
   making 116
   necklace, assembling from
      beads 124–126
   textile 117

Lace, machine-made 93,
   112–115

Lacing 136
Landscape as inspiration 27–30
Last, Jenni *11*
Lee, Eleanor *84*
Lemon, Jane *88*
Linear stitches 66, 67, 70
Linen threads 22

Machine embroidery
  appliqué, incorporating
    102–104
  flower shapes *104*
  hand-stitching, incorporating
    104
  lace 112–115
  materials and equipment for 95
  panel 105–107
  popularity of 12, 94
  starting 96, 97
  textures 98–102
  transparent fabrics, on
    108–111
Machine quilting 86, 87
Magazine papers 15
Mary Queen of Scots *88*
Materials
  design, for 15–17
  fabrics 19–21
  machine embroidery, for 95
  threads 22, 23
Matisse, Henri
  Open Window at Collioure 37
Middle Ages, embroidery in 8
Mills, Eleri *13*
Monet, Claude
  Rouen Cathedral paintings *37*
Morell, Luigia *9*
Mounting 135
Museum studies as inspiration 35

Needles 24, 95
Net embroidery 110, 111

Oil pastels 16
Open Window at Collioure 37
Oxburgh Hangings *88*

Pastels 16
Pencils 15
  charcoal 16
  coloured 16

embroidery transfer 24
Painting exercises 48
Paints
  fabric *see* Fabric paints
  transfer 55
  types of 17
Paper, selection of 15
Pattern stitches 66, 69, 72, 73
Pearman, Wendy *32*

Quilter's pen 24
Quilting
  cushion cover 84
  designs 81
  development of 80
  English 81–83, *82*
  Italian 85
  machine, by 86, 87
  trapunto 86
  uses 80
  waistcoat *81*

Rayon threads 22
Renaissance, embroidery in 8
Resist, using 53
Rubbings 34

Sanderson, Elizabeth *81*
Scissors 24
Seurat, Georges 73
Sewing equipment 24, 25
Shadow quilting 108, 109
Shreeve, Alison *72*
Silk
  China, use in 10
  threads 22
Silver Depths of Stillness Lie, The
  13
Sketchbook 15
Sketching 48
Stitches
  backstitch 67
  bullion knots 68
  buttonhole stitch 64, 65
  buttonhole wheels 65, 68
  cable stitch 100
  chain stitch 67
  common stitches 58
  complex 60
  couching 67, 100, 101
  counted thread *58*

countries, associated with 60
cross stitch 69
detached chain 69
direction, varying 63
effects of 66
eyelets 69, 72, 73
fly stitch 62, 63
free running stitch 97
French knots 68
running stitch 67
seeding stitches *51, 61,* 69, 72
simple 58, 60
small garden picture 74–77
stem stitch 67
straight stitches *61*
velvet stitch 68
whip stitch 98, *98*
zigzag stitch 97
Swancutt, Kay *61*
Syon Cope, The *9*

Tacking through tissue 57
Tailor's chalk 24
Tambour work
  muslin, use of 10
Textural stitches 66, 68, 71
Texture
  landscape, of 31–34
  machine embroidery, in
    98–101
Threads
  different, stitching in 63
  machine embroidery, for 95
  quilting, for 83, 85
  types of 22, *23*
Tracing paper 15
Transfer crayons 18, 55
Transfer paints 18, 54
Trapunto quilting 86
Tuckwell, Stephanie *13*
Tuscan Study 11
Twydell, Fay *60*

Walker, Julia *82*
Warren, Verina *13*
Watercolour paints 17
Watercolour paper 15
Water-erasable marker 24
Wool
  threads 22
  use of 10